THE
WORLD'S WEIRDEST
PLACES

by
Nick Redfern

New Page Books
A Division of The Career Press, Inc.
Pompton Plains, NJ

THE WORLD'S WEIRDEST PLACES
EDITED AND TYPESET BY NICOLE DEFELICE
Cover design by Wes Youssi/M80 Branding
Printed in the U.S.A.

To order this title, please call toll-free 1-800-CAREER-1 (NJ and Canada: 201-848-0310) to order using VISA or MasterCard, or for further information on books from Career Press.

The Career Press, Inc.
220 West Parkway, Unit 12
Pompton Plains, NJ 07444
www.careerpress.com
www.newpagebooks.com

Library of Congress Cataloging-in-Publication Data

Redfern, Nicholas, 1964-
    The world's weirdest places / by Nick Redfern.
            p. cm.
    Includes bibliographical references (p.   ) and index.
    ISBN 978-1-60163-237-1 -- ISBN 978-1-60163-562-4 (ebook)
            1. Parapsychology and geography. 2. Geography--
Miscellanea. 3. Haunted places--Miscellanea. 4. Curiosities and
wonders--Miscellanea. I. Title.

BF1045.G46R44 2012
001.94--dc23

                                                          2012019954

Acknowledgments

I would like to offer my very sincere thanks and deep appreciation to everyone at New Page Books and Career Press, particularly, Michael Pye, Laurie Kelly-Pye, Kirsten Dalley, Nicole DeFelice, Gina Talucci, Jeff Piasky, and Adam Schwartz; and to all the staff at Warwick Associates for their fine promotion and publicity campaigns. I would also like to say a very big thank you to my literary agent, Lisa Hagan, for all her hard work and help.

Contents

Introduction

I have a trio of questions for you, the discerning connoisseur of distinct high strangeness. If someone gets a fleeting glance of a UFO soaring across the skies of New York, does that make the Big Apple weird? If a Bigfoot briefly and enigmatically appears in the thick forests outside of Seattle, does that make the city weird? And if a chain-rattling specter materializes for a second or two on the grounds of Buckingham Palace in London, does that make the residence of Queen Elizabeth II weird? The answer to all three is no, it does not. What we have in each of these instances is a singular, strange event that has occurred in one particular locale. But, by definition, the place itself is not weird. Only the thing that decided to put in a one-time, brief appearance was weird. That is not always the case, however. In many instances, it *is* the place itself that is weird, not just the mysterious phenomena that manifest in its midst.

If that same Bigfoot, UFO, or chain-rattling ghost all appeared in one particular, concise location, time and again (possibly even for centuries), along with a fantastic range of other bizarre things, such as lake-monsters, poltergeists, strange energies and vortexes, werewolves, occult activity, aliens, and enigmatic entities (including fairies, elves, and goblins), then this is all highly suggestive that the place is truly weird in the extreme! But the definition of that very emotive word—*weird*—is most certainly wide open to interpretation. For some, it may simply mean odd or eccentric. For others, it might imply terror, fear, panic, and sheer, unrelenting horror. A significant number of people might be inclined to suggest the word equates to unspeakable foulness and revulsion of the highest order; the type of awful thing that lurks in the shadows of the woods on the proverbial dark and stormy night. Or, that it's a most apt term to use when describing matters of a supernatural or occult nature, such as life after death, alien encounters, and fantastic monsters. And that's what you get in *The World's Weirdest Places*: a study of unrelenting weirdness, in all its many and varied forms, guises, and definitions, throughout recorded history, and at numerous locations worldwide.

In the pages of this book, you will learn the startling truths of the many amazing, paranormal, and uncanny hot-spots that pepper our planet, as well as the terrible things that call such places their permanent homes. They are hot-spots that extend from the United States to Russia, from Scotland to Canada, from the Philippines to England, from Iceland to Australia, from Guyana to the Solomon Islands, and from just about anywhere and everywhere else in between, too.

In a book like this, one cannot please everyone when it comes to the locations selected and singled out for study. Some readers may wonder why, for example, I have not included such mystery-filled, famous places as Stonehenge, England; the Giza Necropolis at Cairo, Egypt; and Point Pleasant, West Virginia—home to the glowing-eyed, winged nightmare made infamous in John Keel's book, and subsequent movie of the same name, *The Mothman Prophecies*. The answer is very simple: these haunts, and many others, have been covered in countless other titles and, arguably, to the point of near saturation. So, instead, what you get in the pages of this book are my personal favorite supernatural sites, some well-known—but with a new spin placed upon them—and many far less so, but all of them undeniably and unsettlingly weird.

1

Bermuda Triangle, North Atlantic Ocean

Extending from Bermuda in the north to southern Florida, and then east to a point through the Bahamas past Puerto Rico and then back again to Bermuda, is a truly ominous realm of wild, churning, and turbulent waters known infamously as the Bermuda Triangle, a permanent fixture in the western part of the North Atlantic Ocean, and one that has become renowned for the hundreds of aircraft, ships, boats, and unfortunate souls who have disappeared in the area without trace. Down-to-earth explanations for such vanishings most certainly proliferate. Compass malfunctions, disorientation, sudden and violent bouts of severe weather, mechanical and electrical failure, and pilot error are just some of the conventional theories that have been offered as answers relative to why there have been so many disappearances in such a clearly delineated area. But not everyone is quite so sure that those particular theories provide all the clues to solving the maritime mystery.

In December 1945, five U.S. Navy Avenger aircraft disappeared in the Bermuda Triangle. (copyright United States Navy)

On numerous occasions, UFOs have been seen in the area. There is talk of high-level government conspiracies to hide the truth of alien kidnappings in the Triangle. Some researchers of the conundrum suspect the still-working remains of fantastic technologies that the people of the fabled land of Atlantis managed to successfully harness, before their violent destruction, are squarely to blame. The predations of Godzilla-sized sea-serpents and the effects of strange electromagnetic disturbances are also all among the many and varied controversial candidates for the disappearances. And with the theories outlined, let's take a look at some of the more intriguing and hard-to-reconcile cases.

In terms of boats, ships, and their crews disappearing in the area, the list is impressive; far too impressive to list in total, but three choice accounts will provide a good indication of what one might expect to encounter on a journey into those ominous waters. On March 14, 1918, the *USS Cyclops* was Baltimore-bound from Barbados, when it disappeared into complete oblivion. With the loss of more than 300 lives, ostensibly as a result of structural failure, many have quietly pointed fingers in the direction of the Triangle and its attendant puzzles. Two years later, a schooner, the *Carroll A. Deering*, became a victim of that cursed area of ocean while en-route to Rio de Janeiro, Brazil, from its starting point at Norfolk, Virginia. What made this affair particularly notable is that although the ship was found, the crew was not. Each and every one had vanished forever.

Moving on, in early February 1963, after setting off from Beaumont, Texas, the *SS Marine Sulphur Queen* and its nearly 40 crew members took their very last breaths while negotiating those harsh, uninviting seas. All was well for a few days, as the craft headed toward Norfolk, Virginia. But by February 6th, the ship was a day overdue. The Coast Guard quickly swung into action, but despite extensive, two-week searches in the Florida Straits, only a small amount of debris and a single life jacket were found. The *SS Marine Sulphur Queen* and its men were gone—the result of poor structural issues, or the mysterious might of the Bermuda Triangle? Decades later, the question still remains unanswered.

Having looked at the waters *below* the Bermuda Triangle, what about the skies *above* it? They, too, have come face to face with the wrath of the deadly phenomenon.

It is an inevitable fact of life that in a carnage-filled conflict such as that of World War II, fatalities are going to be huge. It is also a fact that of the many who lost their lives during the war, some who died in battle were gone forever—their bodies never located or identified. However, there occurred during World War II a host of perplexing disappearances of military personnel that cannot be explained quite so easily. And guess where some of those more profound disappearances occurred? Moreover, there are those that, in the same time frame, almost became victims of the Bermuda Triangle but at the very last moment, were bafflingly spared a deadly fate. Let us take a look at a few such cases from this war-torn era.

One of those who luckily survived a dicey flight through the Bermuda Triangle in World War II was Lieutenant Robert Ulmer, who, in November 1943, was flying over the area in a Boeing B-24, at a height of 9,000 feet on a clear and bright day. Suddenly, Ulmer noticed with horror that his on-board instrumentation was malfunctioning wildly— something that has been recorded on numerous occasions in this most perplexing part of the world. More alarmingly, the plane shook violently and plummeted a stomach-churning 4,000 feet.

Realizing that the B-24 was utterly out of control, Ulmer knew he had only one option available to him: The crew was ordered to immediately bail out. Curiously, however, after the men parachuted from the aircraft, it then righted itself and proceeded to stay in the air for a startling 1,500 miles and even crossed the Gulf of Mexico before finally slamming into a mountain. It is also important to note that the crew was of the opinion that the area where their mysterious encounter occurred was one of undeniable weirdness. In 1976, Dr. Robert Rigby, who had been the navigator on that very flight, went public, and offered his firm opinion that mysterious forces dominate the area and that, as far his November 1943 experience was concerned, no regular answer to explain the near-catastrophic event would ever satisfy him.

Not everyone who dared cross the Bermuda Triangle during World War II was quite as fortunate as Rigby and Ulmer, however. In December 1944, a group of seven U.S. bombers stopped off at Kindley Field, Bermuda, while flying to Italy to act as replacements for the battle-scarred 15th Air Force. With refueling complete and the crews fully rested, the aircraft then took to the skies once more. The Bermuda Triangle lay only a few miles ahead.

Without warning, on entering the treacherous realm, the flight encountered a series of strange and terrifying weather phenomena that literally appeared out of nowhere. Panic-stricken and unable to fully comprehend what was going on, the crews could only fight valiantly to control their aircraft as a mysterious and violent turbulence buffeted them high into the skies and then plunged them hundreds of feet in mere seconds. So devastating was the experience that five of the aircraft vanished into oblivion. The Triangle had coldly claimed yet more lives, and it displayed no signs of stopping.

Whether by chance or design, such incidents proliferated in the post-1944 era. In January 1945, a B-25 bomber was lost between Bermuda and the Azores with a crew of nine; in March of that same year, a Commander Billson dared to take on the might of the Triangle. Interestingly, but highly disturbing for Billson, both the radio compass and the magnetic compass of his aircraft began to spin wildly until he was finally out of the Bermuda Triangle and normality quickly returned.

But what of more modern-day encounters in the Bermuda Triangle? Do they exist? Most certainly. Since 1991, numerous airliners—hit by sudden, out of the blue aerial turbulence and severe electronic interference—have been forced to make emergency landings in the very area over which the Bermuda Triangle is claimed to hold supernatural sway. An American Airlines Airbus in 1991, another in 1993, a Continental Airlines plane two years later, and an additional Airbus in 1996, were all such victims. And, in 2008, the crew and 10 passengers of a Trislander aircraft all met mysterious and never-resolved ends when they placed a mayday call while Bahamas-bound. But, why should such there have been so many vanishings and mechanical malfunctions, and in such strange fashions, at all? Let's take a deeper look at those theories outlined at the start of this chapter. We begin by taking careful and cautious steps into the cosmic domain of Unidentified Flying Objects.

One famous case that many researchers have placed firmly in a UFO setting was the vanishing of five U.S. Navy *Avenger* aircraft known as Flight 19 on the afternoon of December 5, 1945. No prizes for guessing the name of the strange region that the 14 men of Flight 19 were passing through at the time of the large-scale disappearance. No provable explanation as to why all five aircraft should have seemingly departed this world without a trace was ever forthcoming. However, the official transcript of the conversation between Flight 19 and base personnel at the Naval Air Station at Fort Lauderdale, Florida, that appears in the U.S. Navy's official report on the case, strongly suggests there was profound weirdness afoot on that deadly day when the entire flight became totally lost and disoriented.

As the official record makes abundantly clear, at around 3:45 p.m., the flight leader radioed a panicky message to Fort Lauderdale that the whole squadron appeared to be off-course and had totally lost sight of land. In response to a request for his position, the leader made a chilling comment: his voice now bordering on hysteria, he admitted that he had no idea of his position—*at all.* And, incredibly, neither did any of the additional crew members. Each and every one of them was in a state of confusion and calamity above waters that they should easily have recognized, but, clearly did not. Then the conversation turned downright ominous and bizarre.

The flight leader claimed not only to be unable to find west—which would have taken his team back to the safety and shores of the U.S. mainland—but stated that the ocean looked strange and not as it should, words that are admittedly wide open to interpretation but intriguing, nevertheless. And, as the disastrous situation continued, so the crews became more and more confused. Flight 19's last officially recorded words before they were gone forever: "We are completely lost" (Berlitz).

They were never heard from again; any of them. Case closed. Or is it? I use the term "last, officially recorded words" with very good reason. *Unofficially*, these were *not* the last words of the crew. In the late 1960s, when Bermuda Triangle-based research was reaching new heights, rumors began to circulate suggesting that a ham radio operator in the area had picked up a final few words from one of the disoriented crew on that strange afternoon in December 1945. His alleged screamed message, suggesting a potential UFO link to the mystery of the Bermuda Triangle, is forever etched in sensational legend: "Don't come after me! They look like they are from outer space! Don't come after me" (Bateman)!

And there's one final matter to consider, too, on this unsettling incident: When it became apparent that Flight 19 was in trouble, a number of aircraft quickly took to the skies in hopes of finding the crews and successfully guiding them back to base. One of those same aircraft was a Martin PBM 5 *Mariner* plane from Banana River Naval Air Station. Its 13-man crew, acutely aware of what was at stake, were fired up and ready to help in any way they could. Unfortunately, they did not. What they did do, however, was vanish forever, just like the doomed pilots for whom they were searching. Two disappearances, both in one day, and neither ever solved. When it comes to the Bermuda Triangle and the attendant stories that surround it, there can be no doubt that the saga of Flight 19 is one that made many a soul a firm believer. And the potential UFO links to the Bermuda Triangle continued.

Oceanographer Dr. Manson Valentine, who deeply studied the mysteries of the Bermuda Triangle, as well as numerous UFO encounters within its very borders, had a notable answer to why there seemed to be such a proliferation of flying saucer-type reports in the area. His response: intelligent creatures from a planet, or even planets, far away were not only stealthily checking out our world and our scientific progress, but were possibly callously kidnapping unsuspecting humans, too, and very possibly from within the depths of the Bermuda Triangle. Interestingly, Valentine was also of the opinion that what he described as energy-centers built in the fog-shrouded past by advanced civilizations—human, extraterrestrial, or a combination of both—existed far below the waters of the Triangle and that these same energy-centers, to which we shall return shortly, were still operating and directly responsible for at least some of the disastrous effects on the navigation equipment of both aircraft and ships.

One particularly significant case involving a craft of unknown origin occurred in April 1973 when a Captain Dan Delmonico, a calm and collected character with a fine reputation for being grounded and logical, had an encounter that could be considered anything but grounded and logical. It was around 4 p.m., while negotiating the waters of the Gulf Stream, specifically between Great Isaac Light, north of Bimini, and Miami, when Delmonico was amazed by the sight of a large cigar-shaped object—nearly 200 feet in length, gray in color, and with rounded ends—which shot through the water. Who, or what, piloted the strange submersible remains unknown.

Unidentified craft of the skies and seas aside, let us now take a trip back in time and to a legendary and ancient body of people whose lasting legacies may offer a wildly alternative answer to the puzzle.

Born in 1877, Edgar Cayce was, without doubt, one of the United States' most famous of all psychics. He still retains a massive and faithful following long after his death in 1945 at the age of 67. One of Cayce's favorite subjects just happened to be that of the renowned land of Atlantis, and its equally renowned people—first referred to in the writings of Plato around 360 BC. According to Cayce's beliefs, in the very distant past, a series of catastrophic events—including one akin to a land-engulfing biblical flood—irreversibly decimated the Atlantean society, wherever it might have been situated. And, numerous parts of the world have been suggested as viable candidates for Atlantis, including the Atlantic Ocean, the Mediterranean, the Canary Islands, the Azores, and many more. Notably, Cayce came to accept that Atlantis existed somewhere off the coast of Florida. Or, Bermuda Triangle territory. Cayce was also sure of the outcome of the disaster that fell upon the people of Atlantis: The survivors were forced to start anew in parts foreign and exotic. One of those locations, maintained Cayce, was Egypt. Thus, in Cayce's mind, it was the Atlanteans who brought the astonishing technology to early Egypt that eventually allowed for the creation of the Sphinx and the pyramids.

Cayce also believed that the Atlanteans possessed what he referred to as Fire Crystals—unimaginably powerful crystals that could be harnessed as a form of destructive energy. When that energy was directed, controlled, and used in the right way—just like atomic energy and electricity—it proved to be a godsend for the Atlanteans. But, said Cayce, after the destruction of Atlantis, the old energy-driven technologies survived, and occasionally, their mighty powers are still unleashed to this day, thus wreaking havoc on whatever happens to be in their way—a ship sailing the sea or an aircraft in the sky. This sounds uncannily like the conclusions of oceanographer Dr. Manson Valentine, who referred to the possible existence of ancient centers of energy within the Bermuda Triangle.

As for the admittedly ingenious sea-serpent suggestion, such beasts would have to be truly immense to sink the *USS Cyclops* in 1918 or bring down something such as Flight 19 in 1945. But maybe we should not rush to judgment quite so fast. On this very matter, it is worth noting that, as now-declassified official British Admiralty files reveal, in December 1857, the crew of the 1,063-ton ship the *Castilan*, sighted near the Atlantic island of St. Helena what was described by the ship's captain, George Henry Harrington, and his crew as a leviathan of the deep in excess of an amazing 500 feet in length! A sea-serpent-type beast of such mammoth proportions could, most would probably agree, wreak untold havoc, death, and destruction on a crew of terrified sailors and their puny ship.

Whether due to marauding monsters, ancient energy sources built by the people of now-extinct Atlantis, or extraterrestrial kidnappers from the stars, the collective events in question ensure the legend of the Bermuda Triangle lives on, even if, unfortunately, many of those that have traveled its waters and skies have not done likewise.

Now, with the mysteries of the Bermuda Triangle described and dissected, it's time for a complete change of track as we take a transatlantic trip to the steep and sinister slopes of a certain mysterious mountain range in North Wales, where equally weird, but very different, things lurk.

2

Berwyn Mountains, Wales

Dominating much of northeast Wales is a huge and lonely mountain range known as the Berwyns. Amongst its most eye-catching and imposing peaks are Cadair Bronwen, which stands at 2,572 feet; the 2,723-foot-high Cadair Berwyn; and the 2,712-foot-tall Moel Sych. And when I say it's a lonely location, I do not exaggerate. Even today, in the bustling 21st century, only one road, the B4391, provides access to anyone who might wish to travel the lengths of the vast range from village to village. No wonder, then, with a distinct lack of roads and nothing but mountains for just about as far as the eye can see, many of the surrounding little hamlets remain largely unchanged for centuries and curiously detached from the outside world and its fast-paced existence.

Even the name of the range is steeped in ancient folklore, magic, and mystery. T. Gwynn Jones, a novelist, poet, journalist, and the author of the acclaimed book *Welsh Folklore and Welsh Folk-custom*, developed an intriguing theory to explain the origin of the word *berwyn*. Jones believed it was a distorted combination of *bre*, meaning hill, and

Gwyn, the latter a reference to Gwyn ab Nudd, a legendary, and possibly mythological, Welsh king. He is described as having been a mighty and fearless character—one who appears in a number of ancient stories relative to the famous King Arthur—and a warlord who reigned over a certain race of people called the Tylwyth teg. Better known as the fairy folk, they made their magical home in the land of Annwn, which translates as the Otherworld. And Gwyn ab Nudd was most assuredly not a ruler with whom to cross paths.

The Wild Hunt: A supernatural spectacle of the Berwyn Mountains (Friedrich Wilhelm Malmstrom, 1882)

Before Christianity was brought to the British Isles, there was a widespread belief that the Norse god, Odin, soared across the skies of the nation on cold and stormy nights, accompanied by a terrifying pack of supernatural dogs that would bay at the heels of Odin's equally supernatural stallion. To see the horrific spectacle might result in the unfortunate witness being dragged away to a world of unearthly proportions, while to try and engage Odin in conversation meant certain death for anyone foolhardy enough to even attempt such an act. Thus was born the legend of what has become known as the Wild Hunt. Over time, however, and as beliefs changed and mutated, Odin was relegated to the sidelines, and other supernatural figures began to feature prominently in the old tales, including Satan himself, as well as a variety of demons, fairies, and the souls of the dead.

For the people of the Berwyn Mountains, however, it was Gwyn ab Nudd who became, we might say, the leader of the pack. The unstoppable warrior, then, was a character both revered and feared in equal measures, and particularly so when he led his crazed and infernal howling hounds across the Berwyn heavens on chilled winter eves. As for the Otherworld—Annwn—which became so associated with Gwyn ab Nudd, it was a curious and magical place; it was one where time stood still, people never aged, youth and beauty were staple fixtures, food was in abundance, and disease and illness were non-existent. While most people might scoff at such tales, in and around the Berwyns the traditions and beliefs of old are not so easily dismissed or discarded. Even today, for many, and particularly those people whose families have lived in the area for generations, the ancient king still surfs the skies above, his terrible pack of deadly dogs forever following hot on his heels.

From the skies of the Berwyns, we now have to turn our attention to the mysterious waters below them. Loch Ness, Scotland, is home to the legendary lake-monster called Nessie. Lake Okanagan, in British Columbia, Canada, boasts its own water-based beast, Ogopogo. In the depths of Lake Champlain, Vermont, lurks a serpentine, snake-like creature dubbed Champ. And in Lake Bala—or Llyn Tegid, to give it its Welsh wording—swims Teggie. The lake, the largest natural body of water in Wales, and one long-rumored to be bottomless, is barely a stone's throw from the fringes of the Berwyn Mountains, making the matter more intriguing. So, what do we know for sure about Teggie? Well, one of the most notable and provable things is that Lake Bala is home to the Gwyniad, a type of prehistoric fish that is not found anywhere else in the world. So, with one ancient creature in residence at the lake, might there also be a second one, perhaps one far bigger and much more menacing than the relatively small Gwyniad?

Most perplexing about Teggie is that the sightings and legends of the animal only began in and around the mid-to-late 1910s and early 1920s, which surely begs a couple of important questions: If the beast was not in residence prior to that period, then how did it get into the lake in the first place? And from where, exactly, did it come? Some Berwyn-based folk quietly, and knowingly, suggest the answer can be found in the world of shadowy cover-up and conspiracy.

During World War I, the British military secretly released into Lake Bala a number of large seals—or so local legend and rumor maintains. The covert plan was to strap dummy mines to the animals and then train them to swim headlong at selected targets, such as rowing boats strategically placed in lake. Outside of the lake, the ultimate top-secret goal, when training was complete, was for the mines to be armed and for the seals to attack German warships and blast them to smithereens— and, unfortunately, the seals too. So the theory goes, however, a number of rather astute seals did not take too kindly to being told what to do or being strapped with fake explosives, so they made their escape and ensured they stayed below water as often as possible, and out of the hands of their trainers at pretty much all times. And, eventually, with the clandestine plan seen as not being a viable one after all, the military shut down the program, quietly exited the area, and left the seals behind to swim and live happily ever after in their new home. Thus, in this particular version of events, Teggie and its ilk are actually the descendants of those original wartime-era seals, not marauding lake monsters. Not everyone is quite so sure about that, however. Most certainly, many inhabitants of the Berwyn Mountains aren't.

Stories of gigantic and ferocious pike in the lake, of a size and strength enough to quickly drag a man to his watery death, abound. Others claim to have seen an approximately 8-foot long crocodile-like animal swimming in the water. And there is even an account of something large and terrifying that broke the surface of Lake Bala a number of years ago and literally lifted an unfortunate windsurfer out of the water, tossing him to one side as one might casually swat a fly in flight. Clearly, however, all of these theories for the origin of Teggie cannot be correct. And so the mystery remains, which is very good news for the people of Bala, and particularly the bed-and-breakfast owners, pub landlords, and restaurant staff who derive welcomed income from those who wish to visit the town, check out the lake, and seek out Teggie for themselves.

And now, with water monsters and magical kings of old out of the way, onto the Berwyns' very own equivalent of Roswell. The mountain range boasts a crashed UFO legend. Like its far more famous New Mexico-based equivalent of 1947, it's one that just will not go away.

Back in 1958, a man named Gavin Gibbons wrote a children's science-fiction novel titled *By Space Ship to the Moon,* in which a UFO from another world lands on the 2,713-foot-tall Moel Sych on the Berwyn Mountains. Based on what comes next, one might be very justified in saying that Gibbons was quite the paranormal prophet. It was on the cold winter's night of January 23, 1974, that a curious and still-unresolved incident occurred on the Berwyns. Within the realms where UFO researchers lurk, it is known as the closest thing Britain has to the notorious flying saucer crash at Roswell, New Mexico, in July 1947. Investigative author Andy Roberts, who has spent years diligently and valiantly trying to unravel the many complexities in the controversial story, said concisely: "The claim was that a UFO piloted by extraterrestrials crashed, or was shot down, on the mountain known as Cadair Berwyn and that the alien crew, some still alive, were whisked off to a secret military installation in the south of England for study" (Roberts, 2010).

The secret facility to which Roberts was referring is called Porton Down, a government establishment whose overwhelmingly classified work focuses significantly on lethal viruses, and chemical and biological warfare. The original source of the story, meanwhile, was a North Yorkshire, England, police sergeant named Tony Dodd. With a quarter of a century of service on the force to his credit, Dodd claimed to have met a retired British Army source in 1996 who shared the amazing secrets of an alien.

According to the source (who Dodd gave the pseudonym of James Prescott), at the time of the Berwyn incident in January 1974, he was stationed at a military base in the south of England, the name of which he declined to identify to Dodd. But, he was willing to provide the salient and startling facts relative to what had occurred. Prescott told Dodd that even as early as January 18th it was very obvious that the base was on high-alert—albeit for reasons unknown outside of a small and select elite. Within 24 hours, however, matters changed drastically and

Prescott and his colleagues were ordered to fire up their trucks and head toward the English city of Birmingham.

Then, on arriving in the Birmingham area, they were told to make their way directly to the town of Llangollen, which, just like the Berwyns, is situated in northeast Wales. When the convoy of military trucks got to Llangollen, said Dodd's informant, night had well and truly fallen, and everyone could see that something deeply strange and secret was afoot. Military aircraft and helicopters were criss-crossing the skies over the Berwyns; powerful searchlights lit up Cadair Berwyn, clearly looking for something on the old slopes; and countless British Army personnel were running around in panic. Before Prescott could ask what was afoot, his unit was ordered to hit the road again: to the small village of Llandderfel. Upon their arrival, they were met by another unit that handed over a pair of large, rectangular boxes: "We were at this time warned not to open the boxes, but to proceed to Porton Down and deliver the boxes," said Prescott (Dodd).

Several hours later, the base was finally in sight. Prescott and his comrades were directed to a particular part of the installation where, in the presence of the men, the boxes were carefully opened by Porton Down personnel. According to Prescott, they contained a pair of strange-looking, non-human entities that someone had placed inside decontamination suits. The staff at Porton then began the dicey task of opening the suits. Prescott said that when this action was complete, it became obvious to everyone in attendance that the entities were not from this neighborhood. They weren't even from this world. Prescott added:

> What I saw in the boxes that day made me change my whole concept of life. The bodies were about five to six feet tall, humanoid in shape, but so thin they looked almost skeletal with a covering skin. Although I did not see a craft at the scene of the recovery, I was informed that a large craft had crashed and was recovered by other military units." (*Cosmic Crashes*)

More astounding was what Prescott had kept until last. A few days after the events of January 1974 occurred he had the opportunity to speak with several other colleagues from his own unit who quietly told him they, too, had transported aliens to Porton Down, after they were found on a mountainside right in the heart of the Berwyns. But, there was one amazing difference, revealed Prescott: *"Their cargo was still alive"* (Ibid.).

On that high—and undeniably controversial—note, ends the astonishing tale of James Prescott, one truly of *X-Files* proportions. Today, unfortunately, Tony Dodd is no longer with us, the real identity of James Prescott remains as frustratingly unknown as it was in 1996, and yet another mystery of the Berwyns has taken on proportions both mammoth and legendary. Perhaps, one day, however, we will finally learn the full and startling truths behind the puzzles and secrets that those massive old mountains have carefully concealed for so long.

Speaking of puzzles and secrets, let's go on a long and wild journey back in time and to a ghost-infested, mysterious city that none dare walk by night.

3

Bhangarh, India

Bhangarh is an old, ruined, and undeniably atmospheric city dating back to the 16th century that sits on the edges of the Sariska forestland in the Indian state of Rajasthan. It was founded by the Maharaja Bhagwant Das as a residence for General Raja Man Singh, a powerful warrior who fought under a legendary Indian ruler, Emperor Jalal-ud-Din Muhammad Akbar—without whose might and influence the creation of Bhangarh never would have come to fruition.

A huge, strategically placed fortress was added in 1630, by Chhatar Singh, the son of Madho Singh, and in direct response to an attack by the forces of a rival, nearby kingdom. And, for a while, Bhangarh, and its more than 10,000 buildings was an absolutely bustling metropolis. Surrounded on three sides by large hills and thick undergrowth, and once filled with temples, markets, pavilions, palaces, and throngs of people, Bhangarh was defined by its majestic splendor. *For a while*. Today, Bhangarh is noted for one thing more than anything else: a most distinct and extraordinary lack of any people whatsoever.

25

Emperor Akbar, without whom there would be no ghostly Bhangarh (copyright Manohar, 16th century)

It was in the late 1700s and under very mysterious circumstances that each and every one of the people of Bhangarh fled for pastures new and far, far away. The farther away, the better. The official reason for why the city became so quickly deserted is that a catastrophic famine hit the area out of the blue, one that may have been caused by a fatal disease to the animal population that the city's residents relied upon for food, and from which the people never stood a chance of recovering. As a direct result, one and all were forced to make hasty moves elsewhere. The unofficial reason—which is still widely accepted throughout Rajasthan—as to why Bhangarh became a ghost town is, however, acutely different in nature. There is an overriding belief that a malignant curse was placed upon the city and its inhabitants, one that led to an emergency exodus filled with chaos and fear.

The curse in question was one that instilled deep fear in all those who lived in Bhangarh. It said that anyone who dared not leave would find their souls forever destined and damned to remain trapped after death, never able to move on to the next plane of existence. And the air of paranormal menace that filled the air hundreds of years ago still permeates prominently to this very day. Visitors to Bhangarh tell of a deep, but hard to define sense of foreboding hanging in the air. An atmosphere of profound, eerie unease dominates the crumbling and weather-beaten buildings. Even the Indian government loudly and prominently warns people to stay away from the ruins of the old city after the sun has set. And stories of diabolical, manipulative magic undertaken in the ancient city centuries ago absolutely abound. As for how the curse and the subsequent disappearance of the people of Bhangarh came to be, it is a story dominated by three things: love, lust, and supernatural intrigue.

Beyond any shadow of a doubt, the pride of all Rajasthan and its populace at the time when it was still very much a busy metropolis was a teenage princess, Rani Ratnawati, whose beauty attracted the attention of many, including a skilled magician steeped in the very blackest of all black arts. His name was Singhia Sevra and, by whatever means necessary—fair or foul—he was determined to make Rani his very own. Astutely recognizing that Rani's father would never agree to a union between the pair under *any* circumstances, Sevra knew that he had to find an alternative way to capture the heart and soul of the young princess. But, just like Shakespeare's *Romeo and Juliet*, it was fated to end in tragedy and death for one and all in this soap opera of supernatural proportions.

Sevra secretly took it upon himself to stealthily and regularly follow not only the movements of the princess whenever she left the palace, but of her staff and servants, too. And as a result of secretly acquainting himself with just about all there was to know concerning Rani and those who surrounded her, on one particular day, Sevra pursued the princess and her personal maid to a local market, where the latter was engaged in purchasing a variety of exotic scents and oils for her mistress. Now was the time for Sevra to make his decisive strike for the heart of Princess Rani. Using all the terrible powers of the archaic, paranormal rituals that he had so skillfully learned, the cunning magician quickly cast a dark spell upon one of the bottles of oil. It was a spell ingeniously designed to ensure that when the oil touched the skin of the princess, it would immediately place her under his hypnotic control and allure, and, in an instant, she would fall completely in love with him. Fate, evidently having other plans already in store, did not allow it to work out quite that way, however.

Unbeknownst to Sevra, Rani had heard from both close confidantes and her guards at the palace that the magician wanted her as his own. As a result, she knew exactly who Sevra was, what he looked like, of his plans to make her his, and of his infernal, occult-dominated reputation, too. But there was something else. It was something that not even Sevra could have anticipated or planned for: The princess was also deeply steeped in the teachings of the occult and magical matters. And, fortunately for Rani, one of her royal guards—who was also in attendance in the market at the time—caught sight of Sevra's malevolent and lust-filled eyes as they focused so deeply on the innocent looking bottle of oil. So, Rani and her loyal protector quickly developed a plan to counter that of her cunningly evil admirer. With the oil having been purchased by her maid, the princess took the bottle from her and smashed it down hard upon a large stone block and cast her very own spell to counter that of Sevra. No sooner had the oil hit the block, when Rani's magic began to work its wonders. The tables were about to be turned.

The huge stone suddenly began to roll, at frightening speed, in the direction of the wicked wizard, and slammed into his body, fatally injuring him as it did so. As Sevra lay dying, his chest crushed by the weight of the mighty stone, he just about managed to splutter out a few, final, whispered words. He forever cursed Bhangarh and its people, warning them that death and tragedy for one and all would soon follow. And both did follow, in the following year, when Bhangarh was hit hard in a violent war with an opposing people: the Ajabgarh. It was a war that led to countless deaths, including that of the beautiful, young princess, Rani. And, legend says, the souls of all those violently slaughtered in the confrontation—including both the princess and the evil magician—remain forever trapped amid the deserted ruins of that once renowned city.

In legends like this one, it's fair to say that things are never quite as clear as one might hope them to be. A variation on the story suggests that the evil magician was not Singhia Sevra, but a sorcerer named Amit Yadav, and that the princess was actually a queen named Kanchan Yadav. But, the means by which the evil sorcerer met his bone-crushing end was said to have been very much the same in both tales. And, Amit Yadav, too, had deep words of warning for the queen and the residents of Bhangarh. He is reputed to have offered chilling, final words of dire warning as he breathed his very last: Bhangarh, and each and every one of its people, were doomed. Death, he whispered, was looming large for all. If the story has any degree of truth to it, then Yadav most certainly knew of what he spoke. The following morning, the tale goes, the city was subjected to a storm of apocalyptic proportions that leveled homes, destroyed the queen's palace, and left nothing but death and disaster in its wake.

Then, there is yet *another* variation on the tale. It suggests that the curse placed upon Bhangarh was caused by one Baba Balanath, a deeply spiritual follower of asceticism—or abstinence—whose daily rituals included mediating on a nearby hill. He loudly warned the founders of the city when the construction of Bhangarh was still very much in its infancy that if the shadows of the buildings should ever touch him while he meditated, a terrible end would befall each and every one of those that settled there. Unfortunately for the builders of Bhangarh, and to their everlasting cost, they outright ignored his words, and the city was built to such a height that its shadows did indeed envelope Baba Balanath during the course of his meditations. As a result, and all thanks to the wrath of Balanath, the irreversible countdown to the end duly began.

Whether or not the legends are true, or have even the smallest grain of reality attached to them, the fact is that the stories of the curse, as well as the dire threats of Baba Balanath, Amit Yadav, and Sevra, still very much prevail centuries later. Never, on any occasion, has there been even a single attempt by people to return to the area and make new homes there. Tourists and visitors to the city claim to have heard eerie, unsettling, and hypnotic music emanating from the remains of the old buildings—music that almost exclusively echoes around the area by night. Sightings of spectral figures dancing wildly and almost manically, while resplendent in the regal clothing befitting those that dwelled in Bhangarh when it was at its height are also reported on a regular basis. Even the spirit of Baba Balanath has been seen on occasion—he, too, forever chained to the place where he mediated for so long in his physical life. And even officialdom of present-day India does not dismiss such tales of terror out of hand, either.

As evidence of this, the Archaeological Survey of India (the ASI) has erected a large and prominent sign on the edges of the old, cursed city warning people that entering Bhangarh before sunrise and after sunset is strictly prohibited. Just maybe, the government knows far more about the mysteries of Bhangarh than it cares to publicly admit. Certainly, the whole reason why the sign was erected in the first place was because entire swathes of the Indian military flatly refused to patrol there—to keep vagrants and the like at bay—for fear of becoming the very next victims of the old curse. But, there can be no denying that the city has become a boon for Indian tourism, and the government's employees are most certainly not averse to promoting the deep mystery and reputation surrounding the ruined city for capital gain. As a prime example of this, the 2010 Commonwealth Games were held in Delhi, India, from October 3rd to the 14th, and, wishing to boost revenue from the many visitors flocking to the games, the Rajasthan Tourism Development Corporation (RTDC) specifically included Bhangarh in a package tour for those who might want to take a day off from the sports and see the historical sights of the area. The chairman of the RTDC, Manjit Singh, openly admitted that the location was selected to help boost tourism, but stressed in light-hearted terms that not even the Indian Government could guarantee the spectral dead would put in an appearance for the crowds. But, that does not mean if you dare to wander the old city of Bhangarh and its ruins by night, you won't encounter them...

It's not just cities that are haunted. How about a spooky old castle? Indeed, our next stop in search of the world's weirdest places offers a fascinating look at just such a place and its restless spirits, both human and animal.

4

Carew Castle, Pembrokeshire, Wales

Carew Castle, located in Pembrokeshire, Wales, has an intriguing and notable history. Although built on the orders of Gerald de Windsor around 1100, and expanded upon by Nicholas de Carew in 1270, evidence exists to suggest the area on which the ancient fortress was constructed was seen as having prime strategic and military advantage by Welsh warlords as far back as 20 BC. Today, however, the castle has far stranger residents: a ghostly and ghastly gorilla, a renowned princess, and a spectral, World War II-era airwoman.

Although a number of reports exist (spanning four centuries) of people seeing, hearing, or sensing the presence of a spooky ape at Carew Castle, amongst the biggest questions are: How, and under what particular circumstances, did the legend surface? And, what is true nature of the beast? For the answers, we have to travel back in time to the 1600s and the actions of the castle's then-lord, Sir Roland Rhys, who could boast of being a full-fledged, former pirate.

31

So the tale goes, on one of his sea-fearing adventures, Rhys acquired a Barbary ape—or, given that it is actually a monkey and *not* an ape—a Barbary macaque. Living on Gibraltar, and in the Atlas Mountains of Algeria and Morocco, Barbary apes are not large animals, by any stretch of the imagination. Averaging around only 2 and 1/2 feet in height and 34 pounds in weight when fully grown, there is not much chance of such an animal being mistaken for Bigfoot. Or is there?

As early as 1801 and as late as 1969, witnesses to the Carew creature have described the hairy fiend as a shadowy, bulky, gorilla-like animal, which is absolutely at odds with what the old tales tell us about the nature of the animal that is believed to have provoked the legend in the first place. But let us first return to the saga of Sir Roland Rhys, who—with some hindsight—sounds very much like the cruel and maniacal Hugo Baskerville of *The Hound of the Baskervilles* infamy.

An ill-tempered drunk with a deep propensity for violence, bullying, and cruel humor, Rhys would host huge banquets, invite friends and local dignitaries over to dine with him, and then mercilessly taunt them, goad them, and pummel them with insults. And, more often than not on such nights, he would parade, for one and all to see, his very own macaque, which went by the memorable moniker of Satan. By all accounts, Satan was highly intelligent, devious, cunning, and could eerily mimic Rhys' laughter which he, Satan, would also direct at Rhys' guests—many of whom were highly fearful of the wild beast that would appear in their midst dressed in butler-style, posh garb.

Legend suggests that it was a stormy, wind-filled night when there was a loud and echoing knock on the old, mighty wooden door of Carew Castle. Rhys, blind drunk, stumbled to the door. He was confronted by a Flemish tradesman who, having rented land in the area from Rhys, brought over his rent money, which was then overdue by several days. Or, rather, the man had brought *part* of the money with him. Hard times had befallen the man, and he pleaded with Rhys to be given a few more days to try to get the outstanding payment together. Rhys, unsurprisingly for such a cold-hearted character, was having none of it whatsoever, not only because of the money issue, but also because Rhys's son was seeing the man's daughter, a relationship upon which Rhys deeply frowned. So, he took a most different approach to resolving the matter. It was a terrible and bloody approach, too.

In a fashion that eerily paralleled the scene in *The Hound of the Baskervilles* where Hugo lets loose his pack of hunting dogs on the daughter of a local yeoman who has dared to snub his advances, Rhys loosened the chains that kept the ape from roaming too freely and goaded it to attack the petrified man, which it duly did, savagely tearing into his flesh. Fortunately, the man managed to escape the clutches of the laughing, dwarfish, hairy butler. He staggered out of the door, weak, dizzy, and disoriented from both shock and blood loss, and collapsed in a helpless heap on the grounds of the castle. Even more fortunately, a kindly servant—one hardly enamoured by the violent actions of his master and the hairy fiend—bandaged the man's wounds and gave him shelter in his own quarters until the turbulent storm subsided. But, the night's calamitous events were not yet over.

As the servant helped the man gain his footing and guided him to shelter and safety, loud cries and crazed laughter broke out in the main dining hall. The servant raced to the room and was faced with a terrifying sight: By the time the man flung open the door, Rhys was dead, his throat brutally torn open—virtually identical to Hugo Baskerville, when he was attacked and killed by the glowing-eyed, fiend-dog of the book's title. The body of Satan was burning fiercely in the great, stone fireplace that dominated the room (somewhat appropriately, when one takes into consideration the name of the ape). But, neither ape nor master was destined to stay quiet for long. Even the very grave itself could not contain them. To this day, their hysterical, maniacal cackling and their spectral forms continue to be heard and seen in and around Carew Castle—particularly on wild and windy nights that so closely resemble the long-gone thunderous eve upon which alcohol-fueled Sir Roland Rhys and savage, mad Satan met their infernal, terrible ends.

Whether or not Sir Arthur Conan Doyle took any of his inspiration for *The Hound of the Baskervilles* from the saga of Carew Castle and Sir Roland Rhys is an issue very much beyond the scope of this book. It is worth noting, however, that Doyle *did* incorporate the legend of one Richard Cabell, an evil squire who lived at Brook Manor, north of nearby Buckfastleigh, Devon in the 1600s, into the pages of

Carew Castle, Wales: Home to ghosts of both the human and animal kind (Copyright William Miller, 1838)

his acclaimed novel. And, I will say that the parallels that exist between certain integral parts of both *The Hound of the Baskervilles* and the unsettling saga of Roland Rhys and Satan are uncanny and most certainly worthy of further study and scrutiny. What *is not* beyond the scope of this book, however, is the fact that while a ghostly ape *has* been seen in and around the castle on a number of occasions, its sheer size, shape, bulk, and gait are all at significant odds with what one would see in a small Barbary macaque—whether physical or spectral.

Instead, could it be that the legendary story of Sir Roland and his utterly mad butler/pet was simply an invention to rationalize and explain the presence of an ape-like entity seen in the area that defied any and all conventional explanation? It's a distinct possibility that we cannot dismiss. But, what makes matters even more notable is that this is not the only example of high strangeness at the castle.

Far less-well-known than Sir Roland Rhys' Satan, and, thankfully, nowhere near as crazed and psychotic, are Carew Castle's spirits of the human variety. One of them is said to be that of a certain Princess Nest. The daughter of an 11th-century king, Rhys ap Tewder, she is said to be both beautiful on the inside and outside, and pleasantly welcomes kindred souls to her old abode, just as she did in life. Some assume she is merely a member of the staff dressed in centuries-old garb to entertain the tourists. When Princess Nest vanishes in the blink of an eye, however, such a theory evaporates just about as quickly as she does.

The castle's second resident spooky woman, whose name is unknown, has not been a resident of the old castle for too long; certainly no earlier than the 1940s. This is clearly evidenced by her clothing. According to a handful of witnesses from a London-based history society who saw her ethereal form glide across the castle's grounds in February 2002, she wears a World War II-era Royal Air Force uniform of the Women's Auxiliary Air Force (the WAAF). According to all the eye witnesses, the ghostly woman's form, estimated to be somewhere around 25 years of age, was seen within the shallowest waters of the River Carew, which is overlooked by the castle itself. Quite understandably, the first thought of those walking the grounds was that the woman had fallen in the river, and so several ran to the water's edge to help her, even though she was practically on the riverbank by the time they reached her.

Concerns about the young woman's well-being and whether or not the group could offer any assistance were met with nothing more than a mystifying silence and a slightly unnerving stare. Puzzled, and feeling slightly alarmed for reasons that were intriguingly hard to pinpoint, the group simply stood and looked on as the woman slowly walked onto the grassy land that surrounds the castle, took a look back at the group, and then proceeded to fade away into absolute nothingness. Pandemonium broke out. Some people scattered, others screamed, while the remainder just stood there dumbfounded.

Because the woman's form has now been seen on at least five occasions since 2002, the big questions are: Who is she? Why does she haunt the grounds of Carew Castle? And why did she remain unseen until 2002? The answers to all three are unfortunately unknown; however, it may not be mere coincidence that less than a mile from the castle is Carew Control Tower, which saw considerable action during World War II, was constructed in 1938, and was known throughout the war as Royal Air Force Carew Cheriton.

Notably, there *were* a number of deaths at the base that directly resulted from the turbulent times of the war. On October 1, 1940, one death occurred during a raid by Nazi aircrews. Six months later, on April 15, 1941, 12 personnel lost their lives when the base's sickbay took a direct strike from a powerful German bomb. Then, on September 3, 1943, two aircraft catastrophically collided on the runway, resulting in six deaths. Although the base most certainly had its share of tragedy, none of these events can explain the presence of the ghostly airwoman, for one simple reason: all of those killed in these events were male. Thus, the identity of the mysterious, uniformed woman of the castle remains as enigmatic as does the reason for her paranormal presence. But, should you one day pay a visit to Carew Castle and encounter her supernatural form, well, at least it's a far better option than running into that deranged, violent ape!

Mysterious apes of a supernatural nature aren't exclusive to Carew Castle, however. They have also made the Caucasus Mountains of Eurasia their deadly domain.

5

Caucasus Mountains, Eurasia

Who would ever have thought that an entire range of mountains could be considered definitively weird? Such a claim, as we have seen, can most certainly be made about the Berwyn Mountains of North Wales. But it can also be made about the spectacular Caucasus Mountains situated in Eurasia, between the Caspian Sea and the Black Sea, and which are home to the highest mountain in all of Europe: Mount Elbrus. A beautiful but deadly vampire roams the isolated villages of the massive peaks, intent on seeking out copious amounts of fresh blood to feed and fuel her soulless form. The Almasty, a Caucasus equivalent of the North American Bigfoot, also calls the forests and peaks of the area its home. Tales of still-living groups of Mammoths circulate. And then there are the magic rocks of the mountains, behind which lies a story of horrific proportions.

A North Caucasus town situated in Russia's Kabardino-Balkar Republic, Tyrnyauz has a population of a little more than 20,000. The majority of them are just regular, everyday people. One of them, however, most certainly is not. Its name is the Svokan and it dwells in the heart of the nearby White Rock hills, adjacent to a ragged and bleak group of immense peaks intriguingly known as the Stepmother's Teeth. According to the stories passed down across generations of residents of the town, the Svokan is a gigantic, muscular man-beast, around 20 feet tall, partly covered in white hair, and possessed of a cone-shaped head that is set off by a pair of glowing red eyes and immense fang-like teeth. And, most unfortunate for the people that live in the vicinity, the favorite delicacy of the Svokan just happens to be humans. But, it feasts in a most strange and unearthly manner.

Legend suggests the Svokan is a creature with powerful, magical abilities that know no bounds. For the Svokan, bones, meat, and blood are just not enough. Locals maintain that the beast first snares its prey by hiding out in the woods at night, mimicking the distressed cries of a human baby, and cunningly enticing its victim to follow the sounds. Then, when the unlucky soul is in the dark depths of the forest, utterly disoriented, the Svokan quickly pounces. Not via a savage attack with its teeth and claws, however. Rather, the Svokan casts upon the terrified person a terrible spell that turns them into a small ball of stone, and which the unholy monster then carries back to its dark den in the mountains and stacks alongside numerous other such stones, until hunger strikes. But, there is even more to the curious tale.

After being turned to stone, the soul of the victim remains trapped within the ball until it is fully devoured. At that point, the Svokan is sated, and the person's life-force makes its ethereal transition to heaven or hell. But, if another person finds one of the stones before it is swallowed by the Svokan, and if that same person then prays to God and smashes the stone into tiny pieces, such an act will ensure the Svokan stays hungry, and the souls of both the savior and the victim are forever guaranteed a place at God's side. A nice piece of folktale, to be sure, but is that all there is to it? Quite possibly, no. It's here that we have to turn our attention to a creature known to those who live in the Caucasus Mountains as the Almasty—the Russian equivalent of the Bigfoot of North America and the Abominable Snowman of the Himalayas or, as some suggest, possibly even a form of primitive man.

Jonathan Downes, the director of the British-based Center for Fortean Zoology, one of the few groups in the world dedicated to the full-time study of unknown animals, says of the Almasty: "Opinion is divided upon what these creatures are, or may be. It is tempting to theorize that they may be surviving pockets of our closest relative—the Neanderthal men—who supposedly died out in the later part of the Pleistocene epoch (more familiarly known as the Ice Age) some 200,000 to 30,000 years ago." Downes also notes, however, that some researchers, most notably American anthropologist and cryptozoologist Professor Grover Krantz believed the Almasty to be true humans: surviving tribes of Mesolithic (Stone Age) hunter-gatherers, similar to, but more primitive than, the aboriginal natives of the more obscure parts of South America and southeast Asia. Downes adds: "Whichever hypothesis is true, the concept that primitive humans may have survived until the present day is a startling one; as is the idea that the Caucasus Mountains might be home to a creature similar to the Yeti or Bigfoot" (Redfern, *Wild Man!*).

Yes, such a scenario most certainly is startling; however, it is one bolstered by the fact that numerous reports exist of the creatures seen roaming and foraging in the vast expanses of the Caucasus Mountains. One such beast was seen truly up close and personal in the latter stages of World War II by a man named Erjib Koshokoyev, a resident of the mountains at the time. It was one particular night in October 1944, and Koshokoyev, a policeman, was part of a detachment patrolling local fields and hills on horseback. Suddenly, the horse of the officer leading the group abruptly stopped in its tracks, refusing to move any further. This was not surprising: only a few feet ahead, a large, hairy, man-like beast was voraciously feeding upon a field of hemp!

Quickly realizing it had been seen, the creature bounded away at an extraordinary speed, and headed in the direction of a nearby shepherd's cabin. The police, both amazed and excited, and armed with rifles, were not far behind, however. One even attempted to fell the creature as it ran, but the officer in charge chastised the man and ordered that it be taken alive for transfer to Nalchik, the capital city of the Kabardino-Balkar Republic. So, a daring plan was put swiftly into action. On reaching the cabin, the group quietly and cautiously dismounted, formed a circle around the old building, and were about to fling the door open when the Almasty jumped out from the darkness of the cabin, clearly agitated, and raced back and forth wildly in front of the cabin door, while mumbling unintelligibly and grimacing. The officers formed a line and advanced with a high degree of trepidation. The Almasty was no coward, however. It charged at the men frantically and at an incredible pace, screaming loudly in an animalistic, primal fashion.

The orderly line of policemen was immediately reduced to a chaotic group of frantic, frightened souls unable to stop the wild thing from making good its escape by jumping a ravine and vanishing into the brush surrounding a nearby river. But, fortunately, even those few brief moments had given Koshokoyev a good chance to get a solid look at the mysterious beast. It was, he said, clearly humanoid, nearly 6 and 1/2 feet in height, extremely robust, covered in long, shaggy, red-colored hair, and dressed in what looked like an old, tattered caftan. So, you may ask, how does this tie in with the legend of the man-eating Svokan of the Caucasus Mountains? Let's take a look at what we know for sure.

In the Caucasus Mountains roam vampires and marauding ape-men (Copyright NASA)

In the folktales, the Svokan is a large, wild, man-like beast that lives in the high peaks, just like the Almasty. The Svokan is covered in hair, just like the Almasty. But, what about those victims turned to stone that the Svokan devours? Well, it's most illuminating to note that in the direct vicinity where the Almasty has been seen in the Caucasus Mountains and where Bigfoot has been encountered in the Pacific Northwest forests of the United States, large piles of rocks and stones have very often been found, too. Bigfoot researchers suggest they may be territorial markers, created by the beasts themselves to either attract or warn away others of their kind. Could it be, then, that the old legends suggesting a connection between the Svokan and piles of stone are actually based on people seeing, centuries ago, Almastys constructing stone-based territorial boundary markers high in the mountains? Quite possibly; and, it's very easy to understand how encountering such an immense, primitive-looking beast at a glance on the cold slopes might very quickly provoke stories suggesting a literal, monstrous man-eater was on the loose in the Caucasus Mountains. Thus, in a strange but undoubtedly distorted fashion, the Almasty and the Svokan may very well be one and the same.

Now, let's move on from man-beasts to deadly she-vampires.

Any mention of the word *vampire* inevitably conjures up imagery of the black-cloaked blood-suckers made famous in old monster movies starring Bela Lugosi and Christopher Lee as the legendary Count Dracula, or Hollywood's *Twilight* saga and HBO's *True Blood* series. The vampire, however, is a cold-hearted creature not born out of Tinsel Town, but one that has been with us for thousands of years and one deeply feared within numerous cultures. The ancient Romans and Greeks lived in deathly terror of the Striges, and Norse mythology tells of the horrific Draugr. Madagascar is home to the rampaging Ramanga. Although certain characteristics and traits may change according to region and century, all of these entities have one thing in common: They are supernatural creatures, sometimes—but not exclusively—the dead returned from the grave, and all driven by a voracious and violent need to feed on copious amounts of human blood. And, in view of the world-wide nature of the phenomenon, it's not at all surprising that the Caucasus Mountains should have their very own resident creature of the night, too. It goes by the name of the Morana—which also happens to be the very same title applied to a blood-sucking monstrosity that haunts the Dalmatian area of Croatia.

For the people of the little towns of the mountains, the Morana exclusively appears in the guise of a beautiful maiden. She is not an example of the dead returned, however. No: S*he* is actually an *it*; a supernatural shape-shifter whose real form is definitively devilish. Skin oily and black, a pair of goat-like horns, talons for fingers, and eyes that glow red in hypnotic and enticing style, are amongst its cruel calling cards. But, when feeding time comes around, the demon is replaced by that alluring woman whose spell has ensured doom for the men-folk of the Caucasus Mountains for eons. Although belief in the existence of the Morana is not as strong or known today as it was centuries ago, for many of the people who make their home in the area, many are unable to wholly dismiss or shake off the possibility that the predatory fiend still walks the mountains on cold, dark, windswept nights.

The mammoth was a majestic and legendary creature that roamed the lonely wilds of North America, the vast expanses of Western Europe, and the harsh, frozen lands of northern Russia during the Pleistocene era, and which is generally accepted as having finally become extinct at some time around the end of the last Ice Age. Today, all we have left of this mighty beast are a number of fairly well preserved carcasses found embedded in icy tombs, and the various bone and tusk fragments that still surface from time to time. Could there, however, still possibly be more—maybe even *much* more—just waiting to be uncovered?

For centuries, intriguing and admittedly sensational rumors have surfaced to the effect that in some of the more remote parts of our planet the mammoth just might still exist, blissfully unaware of what such a jaw-dropping revelation would mean to the world's zoological community, if one day fully confirmed. And although such a scenario is certainly deeply controversial in the extreme, and one that is completely derided by mainstream science and zoology, perhaps it is not entirely out of the question.

In the late 19th century, a researcher and adventurer named Bengt Sjogren learned that tales were both wildly and widely circulating in remote parts of Alaska about giant, hairy, tusked creatures that lived deep under cover of the huge, ancient forests that dominated the state. The sensational stories don't end there, however. French charge d'affaire, M. Gallon, was working in Vladivostok in 1946, and revealed that, more than 25 years earlier, he had met with a Russian fur-trapper who claimed to have seen what were described as large, hair-covered elephants residing deep inside the heart of the taiga. Gallon added that the trapper appeared to have no previous knowledge of mammoths and seemingly had no visible reason to fake such a wild and unbelievable story. A further sighting allegedly occurred during World War II when a Soviet Air Force pilot reported seeing a small herd of such creatures while he was flying over the frozen wastelands of Siberia.

But, for our purposes, we have to now focus upon the saga of Grigory Tilov, a mountaineer who maintained he encountered two such creatures in 1936, at the foot of Mount Elbrus—the tallest peak in the Caucasus Mountains at more than 18,000 feet. According to Tilov, who related his story in the early 1960s to Felix Ziegel—a doctor of science at the Moscow Aviation Center, and a man who, in 1967, took part in the Soviet Union's first formal study of the UFO mystery—he was about to scale at least parts of the mountain on one particular morning in the summer of 1936 when he was stopped in his tracks by the jaw-dropping sight of two small mammoths lumbering along at a slow pace, approximately 300 feet from him. Even at that distance, said Tilov, there was no mistaking their unique identity. He quickly pulled out his binoculars for a better look and, sure enough, he was not wrong. The mammoth, believed dead for so long by so many, was still among us; but not, perhaps, for too long.

As the animals got closer—to within about 50 feet—but seemingly paying no attention to the astonished climber, Tilov could see that both mammoths were very thin, displayed evidence of significant hair loss, walked slowly and wearily, and were clearly undernourished. Although Tilov possessed a rifle, he told Ziegel that he never even once thought about using it on what he considered to be a pair of amazing animals that it was a privilege to have encountered. Given their emaciated states, Tilov speculated that perhaps they were the very last of their kind, fated to early deaths from starvation at the foot of the Caucasus Mountains. And, just maybe, he was right.

From man-eating monsters to blood-suckers of the night, and from Bigfoot to animals long past their sell-by date, the Caucasus Mountains have played home to each and every one of them.

Now it's time for a complete change of scenery from frozen mountains and terrible monsters. Are you brave enough to take careful and cautious steps into a scalding hot valley of death?

6

Death Valley, California, USA

Located within California's Mojave Desert, Death Valley is a most apt name for a place that resembles the rugged surface of some far away, battle-scarred planet, and holds the dubious honor of being home to the highest recorded temperature in the western world: an incredible 136° Fahrenheit, noted on July 10, 1913, in the very appropriately named Furnace Creek. It is somewhat ironic that, although Death Valley got its memorable moniker during the famous Gold Rush of 1849, only one death among all of the prospectors eager to seek out gold was actually reported during that turbulent period. Though the name of the valley may be relatively new, the history of the area is most definitely not. For more than 1,000 years, the Timbisha Native Americans have lived in the harsh environs of Death Valley. And, in times both past and present, so have a whole range of things undeniably weird.

One of the strangest of all sagas relative to the mysteries of Death Valley erupted in the summer of 1947, the very same period in which the era of the flying saucer took the entire world by storm. In early August of that year, Howard E. Hill, of Los Angeles, spoke before the city's Transportation Club and told a story of sensational proportions. It was an extravagant tale that described the work of a certain Dr. F. Bruce Russell, a retired Cincinnati, Ohio physician, who claimed to have discovered a series of complex tunnels deep below Death Valley in 1931.

Well, you may justifiably ask, so what? After all, caves, caverns, and underground grottos exist pretty much all around the world, don't they? Yes, they most certainly do. But, there was something very special and unique about these particular tunnels beneath Death Valley. According to the story told to Hill by Russell, the caves contained the skeletons of several gigantic men, each around 9 feet in height, which Russell stumbled upon with a colleague, Dr. Daniel S. Bovee, with whom Russell had worked on archaeological excavations in Mexico several years earlier. And *stumbled upon* is highly apt terminology. Russell reportedly fell headlong into one of the caves when the surface soil gave way beneath him as he was in the middle of busily sinking a shaft for a mining claim.

Hill amazed and hushed the audience of the Transportation Club when he said that the huge figures were dressed in what resembled medium-length jackets and pants, but that seemed to be made out of the hides of animals of unknown origins. Upping the weird stakes even further, Hill said that while deep underground, Russell and Bovee apparently came across what they described as a huge hall, in which were found unspecified devices adorned with markings that befitted the regalia of the Freemasons. More bizarrely, the long-dead remains of both tigers and elephants (or, as was later suggested, the remnants of ancient saber-tooth tigers and mammoths) were also found strewn across the floor of the huge hall.

As for this fantastic, below-surface realm, we're not talking about just a few measly tunnels, either. Hill revealed that estimates suggested there were at least 32 of them, and they ran for an amazing 180 square miles, covering whole swathes of Death Valley and certain parts of southern Nevada. As for the era in which the bodies originated, while no explanation was given as to how Russell had come up with such a figure, he estimated they extended back an incredible 80,000 years, if not longer, Hill told the crowd.

Hardly surprisingly, the local media of the day scoffed, and loudly cited the comments of certain, unnamed professional archaeologists who openly laughed at such a story, assuring anyone and everyone who would listen that the story was nothing but a tall tale. Rather incredibly, but some might say predictably, no one in the professional world of archaeology would even dare take up the challenge to see the incredible evidence for him- or herself, possibly fearful of being viewed as gullible and lacking in credibility if they chose to do so. The result: It was left up to Howard E. Hill to continue to speak on behalf of Dr. Russell—which he certainly did, until the story died a mysterious and sudden death, and Hill, Russell, and Bovee vanished into the shadows (or, perhaps, into the depths of those old caves), never to return.

Though many might be inclined to dismiss such an undeniably controversial report, very similar ones abound from the heart of Death Valley. One such story predated Howard Hill's revelations by 15 years. In 1932, only one year after Russell and Bovee reportedly came across that infamous network of underground tunnels, a large hall, and a multitude of gigantic skeletons, a very similar story surfaced from Bourke Lee, a noted early chronicler of Death Valley history and folklore. According to Lee, he got the story in the late 1920s, which would have placed it several years before the experience of Russell and Bovee, but it must be admitted that both accounts are remarkably alike.

In the story told to Lee by Jack and Bill (possible pseudonyms created to protect the real identities of Lee's sources), the underground realm was discovered after they fell through the surface soil and inadvertently stumbled upon the amazing evidence, just like Russell reportedly did several years later. In this case, however, Jack and Bill plunged into the heart of a vast cavern that seemingly extended for around 20 miles, but which eventually opened up into what could only be described as a massive, spacious city of ancient origins, evoking imagery of ancient Rome. And then there were the bodies. They weren't giant skeletons, however. Rather, they were the remains of several mummified men, all carefully positioned in upright fashion and holding gold-colored spears in their hands

Just about everything in the old, huge city seemed to be constructed out of gold, Bourke was told: walls, tables, floors, huge pillars, and vast doors; it was a prospector's greatest dream come to full fruition. There was even some form of artificial lighting in evidence, too—it appeared to be ingeniously powered by a complex network of underground natural gas. Recognizing the clear importance of the secret world of the distant past they had inadvertently uncovered, Jack and Bill slowly and carefully retraced their steps, and finally managed to clamber their way back to the surface world that had so fortuitously given way beneath them. As to who, or what, the ancient creators of this world may have been, Jack and Bill told Bourke Lee they had no idea at all, but they had every intention of going back and finding out. If they did succeed in penetrating the heart of that old city once again, they may very well have never lived to tell the tale. Despite intensive digging on his part, Lee heard no more from them. And, for that matter, neither did anyone else. Death Valley, perhaps, had no intention of giving up its mysterious secrets of civilizations long gone quite that easily.

Death Valley, California, with one of its famous rolling stones (copyright U.S. National Park Service)

Beyond any shadow of doubt, the most famous of all Death Valley's many mysteries are its rolling stones. For decades, astounded visitors to the valley—and particularly so in the vicinity of an 850-foot-high hillside of dolomite on the southern side of its Racetrack Playa—have come across large stones and rocks that appear to have moved across the desert floor of their own free will and under some perceived, but poorly understood, magical power. Such scenarios and beliefs have gained a great deal of weight by the fact that, behind the same stones and rocks, grooves and tracks are always found—sometimes extending for hundreds of feet, and occasionally even displaying evidence of the rocks having actually flipped over during the course of their curious travels across the harsh lands of Death Valley.

Not everyone who has studied the phenomenon is so sure there is a need to bring matters of a paranormal nature into the equation, however. In the late 1940s, a pair of geologists, Allen Agnew and James McAllister, who had heard stories of the curious stones, headed out to Death Valley to see the evidence and to record and study the available data, as did Dwight Carey and Robert Sharp in 1972, and Professor John Reid in 1995, who took with him a team of students from the University of Massachusetts and Hampshire College. The prevailing theory of geologists who have traveled to the area is that the seemingly baffling movement of the stones can be explained by a phenomenon that, though not supernatural in nature, is still certainly remarkable, and one that requires specific weather patterns to be in place to explain the puzzle.

In essence, it's a theory suggesting that when the clay of the flat desert floor becomes saturated with water, strong gusts of wind, of the type that certainly are in evidence in Death Valley's Racetrack Playa, force the stones along on a thin veneer of water—rather like a small yacht propelled along ocean waters during a storm—and, incredibly, sometimes at speeds reaching those one would expect to see in the average person taking a leisurely jog. Not everyone in the academic community is quite so sure that this particularly theory is a sound one, however. Geologist George M. Stanley, for example, noted in a 1955 paper that some of the sailing stones of Death Valley were of a weight equivalent to that of a fully-grown man—something which made Stanley very doubtful of the idea that the power of the wind would be strong enough to kick-start such large and heavy stones, never mind keep them in constant motion for hundreds of feet, or more, across the valley.

There are other problems, too, when it comes to trying to rationalize the enigma. It's not as if each and every time the weather conditions are perceived as being conducive to such activity that dozens of stones all suddenly begin moving across the desert like an army of dutiful, marching soldiers. Only specific, select stones seem to be targeted by whatever phenomenon is at work, while the rest remain totally unmoved by the experience. Every attempt to capture the movements of the stones on film—usually via time-lapse photography—has ended in complete failure. And, in some cases, the stones have actually done 360 degree turns and headed back in the very direction from which they first originated! The result: despite the down-to-earth opinions of the scientific world, the rolling stones of Death Valley continue to bask in a heady mix of mystery, intrigue, and wonder. As does, as we shall now see, the area's resident population of ghostly camels. Yes, you did read that right....

Back in the mid-1800s, the U.S. Army embarked upon a little-known, but fascinating, project to counter the severe problem of so many of its pack-horses dying in the overwhelming heat of the southwest, and particularly in a certain part of the California desert. Grim statistics made the military realize that trying to protect its horses from the power of the sun was no easy task at even the very best of times, nevermind when they might be required to cross Death Valley. So, instead of trying to find a way to improve the situation for the animals, they decided to try their luck in a distinctly different direction. The plan was to replace the horses with animals far more used to treacherous temperatures: a corps of camels.

For a few years, the Army pondered upon the admittedly novel idea, with some elements of the military perceiving the whole thing as viable, and others seeing it as a distinctly harebrained idea. But, in 1855, matters came to fruition when Congress finally allocated $30,000 to get the program on the move. Certainly not a huge sum of money today, but, back then—more than 150 years ago—it was most definitely enough for Major Henry C. Wayne to put together a team and take a ship, the USS Supply, to Smyrna, an old city on the Aegean Coast of Anatolia, where a deal was made to purchase a herd of camels.

Just under a year later, Wayne's team was back on American soil, as were the four-legged, now-legal aliens from afar. During the course of the years immediately following, further overseas purchases of camels were made, and they were all routinely used by the military in areas of the United States where dangerously high temperatures and a lack of regular water were always the order of the day. That situation changed drastically in 1861, however, with the outbreak of the American Civil War.

During the four-year-long conflict, in which North and South fought violently against each other, food reserves fell dramatically and soldiers did whatever had to be done to survive—which, on occasion, included slaughtering sizeable numbers of camels for their abundant supplies of meat. But, rescue was at hand. Some of the camels were spared death and transferred to circuses and zoos. Others, however, were clandestinely released into the heart of the desert wilderness—usually during the dead of night—by those in the military who had not just the task of looking after the camels, but who had grown to love them, much as one would a pet dog or cat. Far better to give the camels at least a chance of freedom than to have them end up on someone's dinner plate, it was reasoned. And there is good evidence that the camels in question not only survived in their new wild environment of the southwest, but thrived, too. Certainly, sightings of camels in the Unites States continued for decades—with the last reliable report surfacing from Douglas, Texas, in 1941. Or, it's more correct to say that the 1941 date marked the final sighting of a *living*, wild camel in the United States' southwest. Now we have to turn our attentions away from the living to the dead.

From mid-1951 comes the story of one Fat Mack Mahoney, a prospector working in Death Valley who claimed to have seen a herd of seven camels roaming leisurely through the desert one scalding weekday afternoon. For Fat Mack, just seeing the camels was astonishing enough; but watching them then dematerialize and vanish into a hazy green fog that came out of nowhere, was even more so. Mahoney, who told his story in the early 1960s to a legendary collector and writer of paranormal tales, Frank Edwards, stood by his tale until his dying day in 1972.

A somewhat similar tale surfaced from, of all places, the home of the rolling stones, Racetrack Playa, in 1962. The witness, Wendell Bishop, was actually there to hopefully catch sight of some of the rocks in action, so to speak. It's deeply ironic, however, that he traveled to Death Valley to find one mystery, and ended up encountering a totally different one. In Bishop's case, while roaming around the area, he was floored by the sight of a solitary camel standing in a small gulley. More incredibly, sitting atop the beast was a man dressed in a Confederate army uniform. Neither camel nor rider seemed to see Bishop, both remained rigidly still, and the only response to Bishop's questions concerning what on earth man and beast were doing in the middle of Death Valley was complete silence. But, Bishop did, eventually, get an answer of sorts. After a couple of minutes of loudly and somewhat worriedly stammering out questions from a distance of about 50 feet, Bishop was shocked to the core by the sight of the animal and its rider suddenly dissolving into absolute nothingness. For years, Bishop kept silent, only telling his wife, who finally went public with the story decades later. If you care to ask today, the U.S. Army will tell you that its camels—all of them, whether in Death Valley or elsewhere—are very long dead and gone.

And if a valley of death isn't enough to deal with, now it's time to find out what lurks in a dark domain named after the Devil himself.

7

Devil's Gate Dam, California, USA

The unusually named Marvel Whiteside Parsons was born on October 2, 1914, in Los Angeles, California to parents Marvel, Sr., and Ruth. After an acrimonious divorce, a year later, however, Ruth, wishing to totally walk away from her old life with an adulterous husband, refused to acknowledge her beloved son by the same first-name as that of her ex, and duly began referring to him as John. Eventually that gave way to the nickname Jack. Jack Parsons would become one of the founding fathers of American rocketry and a noted occultist who hung out at one of the truly weirdest of all places: the ominously named Devil's Gate Dam, situated in the heart of Pasadena. But, before we get to the paranormal-soaked place in question, a bit more about the man, himself, is required.

An absolute genius in the burgeoning field of rocket-based research from the mid 1930s on, Jack Parsons has a huge crater named in his honor. It can be found on the far side of the Moon. For decades, his very own company, the Aerojet Corporation, constructed the solid-fuel rocket boosters that were integral parts of NASA's Space Shuttle fleet.

And, on each and every Halloween, NASA's Jet Propulsion Laboratory (JPL) celebrates what it has come to term as Nativity Day. It is on this particular date—which, students of the occult believe was originally meant to honor the dead, and which has its origins in matters of a pagan and ancient Celtic nature—that the JPL pays deep homage to Parsons and his colleagues from the formative years of rocketry. Such is the extent to which Parsons is revered within NASA there is an enduring joke that JPL should really stand for *Jack Parsons Lives* or *Jack Parsons Laboratory*.

Devil's Gate Dam: A hotbed of paranormal activity (copyright Nick Redfern)

Parsons was also a dedicated follower of the occult teachings of legendary and infamous Aleister "the Great Beast" Crowley, who attempted to invoke the presence and protection of the Greek god, Pan, before each and every rocket flight, as part of a lengthy ritual designed to ensure a successful mission, and a man rumored to have had sexual tendencies that brought him far too close for comfort to his own mother and the family dog (even, some said, at the same time!). This makes NASA's near-worship of Parsons even more intriguing. But, most intriguing of all is the place from where much of Parsons's initial rocket-based experimentation was undertaken. It's time for us to take a trip to a particular part of Pasadena that is both unsettling and unnerving. It reeks of hard-to-define negativity, yet is oddly picturesque and enigmatically inviting, too. Its name is Devil's Gate Dam.

It was at the memorably named dam that none other than the Jet Propulsion Laboratory was created back in by 1930 by staff from the California Institute of Technology, or Caltech, as it is most often referred. As for the dam itself, it was built a full decade earlier by engineers of the Los Angeles County Flood Control District. But what was the deal with that name: Devil's Gate Dam? What on earth would have prompted someone to apply such a weird moniker to a place charged with helping to protect the people of Pasadena from potentially disastrous flood waters? The answer is very simple, yet extremely weird, too.

Locating the dam itself is not a problem. It stands out prominently in Pasadena, as much a major, historic landmark as the very nearby Jet Propulsion Laboratory. But, it is not so much the dam itself that is important, but a certain thing that sits near to the base and foundations of the old dam. Stroll along the top of the dam for a couple of hundred yards and you will come to a steep, circling, and dusty pathway. It is a pathway that, if you dare to follow it, will take you down deep into the heart of mysterious woods, thick and mighty old trees, and winding streams, all of which are overlooked by large, brooding hills. Both dark shadows and deep malignancy dominate this near-hidden area, which is part-natural wildness and part-secluded oasis. So, where does the Devil come into all of this?

At the very foot of the dam is a large piece of rock that resembles the face of what many would describe—and *have* described—as a literal demon. Specifically, it is located in a narrow canyon of the Arroyo Seco, a riverbed that runs from the San Gabriel Mountains right into the heart of the Los Angeles basin. And, whether you are a believer in matters demonic or not, that devilish appearance will amaze you as much as it will entrance you. For those of a skeptical nature, the rocky visage can be explained away very simply by a phenomenon called *pareidolia*. This is the means by which the human brain interprets random imagery as having some meaning or significance behind it; the process of seeing faces in clouds being a typical and often-cited example. But, is that really all there is to the stone-faced demon of the dam? Given what we will now learn of the place, maybe we would be wise to suggest that the truth lies in regions and realms far, far removed from, and much, much darker than, the human mind and the complexities of converting clouds into faces.

In 1942, after several years of invoking Pan at the very center of Devil's Gate Dam, and after becoming firmly acquainted with Aleister Crowley, Jack Parsons was chosen by the Great Beast to head the Agape Lodge of the Thelemic Ordo Templi Orientis (O.T.O.) in California. Crowley had dismissed the former head of the group, Wilfred Smith, and Parsons, who revered Crowley, eagerly accepted the position, and embraced Crowley's so-called Thelemic Rituals—the overall aim of which was to ensure the literal creation of a new form of man and the complete obliteration of Christianity. At least some of these particular rituals were carried out under cover of near complete darkness (occasionally, with the benefit of the light of a full moon) at Devil's Gate Dam, throughout much of the 1940s and the very earliest years of the 1950s. And, it can be argued that Parsons's activities brought terrible tragedy to both himself and the very area in which he was dabbling: that damned dam.

The life of Jack Parsons was horrifically snuffed out on June 17, 1952. Following a massive explosion of mercury fulminate in his Pasadena laboratory, Parsons died in absolute agony, fear, and turmoil, his body torn open and his bones shattered by the pulverizing effects of the huge blast. Knowing souls who moved in the same paranormal-themed circles as Parsons said that his relationship to Crowley ensured that something terrible, some dark inhabitant of an even darker realm, came to collect Parsons's soul. Maybe they were right. And perhaps they were also correct when they said that Parsons's longstanding presence at that devilish, rocky face ensured that it, like Parsons himself, was fated to become inextricably linked with nightmarish negativity and death.

Aside from the occult rites, invocations, and rituals undertaken by Parsons and Crowley, Devil's Gate Dam's reputation as a place of both tragic suicide and vicious murder stands out more than any other. The area in question is home to the Colorado Street Bridge, which just so happens to span the Arroyo Seco bed, where Parsons spent a good deal of time on behalf of both Aleister Crowley and following his passion for rockets. And, while uttering the words *Colorado Street Bridge* does not provoke an extreme response in the average person, the nickname that has been applied to the bridge by those who live near it, or who keenly know of its unsettling reputation, most certainly does generate a noticeable response. It is known throughout the area as Suicide Bridge.

Since its construction in 1912, numerous people—the count is now well into three-figures—have hurled themselves off its large expanse to inevitable deaths far below. Jack Parsons wasn't even born in 1912, nevermind when he first set foot on the scene. But, the possibility that Parsons may have gravitated to, and thereafter amplified the negativity at, a place already mired in doom and gloom, is one we should consider. Then there are the terrible murders….

If numerous suicides and occult activity are not enough for you, then read on. Back in the 1950s, and only a few years after Parsons shuffled off to whatever plane of existence a follower of Aleister Crowley is destined to forever find themselves in, Devil's Gate Dam became the site of a number of horrific child murders. Parsons was gone, but the atmosphere of menace most certainly was not going anywhere anytime soon. In August 1956, 13-year-old Donald Lee Baker and 11-year-old Brenda Howell vanished while they were riding their bicycles on land that sits directly behind the dam itself. Police quickly combed the area after the distraught families of Donald and Brenda alerted authorities to the disappearances of their children. The news was not good. In fact, it was without doubt the absolute worst news possible. Both bikes were finally found, as was Brenda's coat. The two children—alive or dead—were never seen again. And that was just the start of things.

Seven months later, Tommy Bowman—only 8 years old—also vanished from the wooded area behind the dam. What made this disappearance so bizarre was that Tommy went missing while hiking with his family. One moment he was there, and the next, to the absolute consternation of his parents, he wasn't. Ever again. Then, three years after Tommy Bowman entered oblivion, so did a young lad named Bruce Kremen.

Although the disappearances of Tommy and Bruce were never satisfactorily resolved, the cases of Donald and Brenda most certainly were. A crazed serial killer, Mack Ray Edwards, finally confessed to their murders, as well as to the deaths of many more children in the vicinity of Devil's Gate Dam. Shockingly, some suggested Edwards may have slaughtered as many as 20 youngsters from 1953 to 1970. Edwards performed only one positive act in his life: He hung himself on October 30, 1971, while serving a life-sentence in San Quentin State Prison for his atrocious crimes.

But, for all the tragedy of the past, it's important to note that the mysteries of Devil's Gate Dam are not solely immersed in decades long gone.

With its miles of surrounding hills and captivating woodland, Devil's Gate Dam is the ideal place to take your dog for a stroll—which is exactly what a man named Bob Jessup did one chilly afternoon in January, 2011. Initially, all was well with Jessup and his faithful hound, and both had a good time wandering the pathways and partaking in some exercise. That is, until they reached that stony, devilish visage. As the pair got within about 40 or 50 feet of the legendary piece of rock, Jessup was frozen to the spot by the terrifying and monstrous screech of…*something.* Ear-piercing and nerve-jangling, it raised the hairs on Jessup's neck and arms, and clearly had a negative effect on his dog, which shot between its master's legs and sat there, its feet firmly planted on the ground.

As this was a late afternoon in January, the sky was already getting noticeably dark, and so Jessup did his very best to peer into the shadows, but could see nothing untoward. That is, until he took a closer look at the rock-face itself. It was then that overwhelming fear gripped Jessup tightly. Climbing the length of the rock was a Lovecraftian-type beast that was white, with very skinny arms and legs, and, incredibly, had a pair of large, bat-like wings protruding from its bony, angular back. Not surprisingly, Jessup simply stood there, his mouth wide open, and his mind full of uncontrollable fear. Suddenly, however, the winged creature turned and glared directly at him, before issuing yet another loud scream and scaling the rock face in a series of curious and ungainly hops and leaps, and finally vanishing over its peak. For Bob Jessup, the harrowing encounter was over and the spell of frozen fear was gone. His nightmares of that harrowing afternoon, however, continued.

Do the dark specters and malevolent machinations of Jack Parsons and Aleister Crowley continue to hang over Devil's Gate Dam to this very day? Why so many suicides in the area? What of the terrible murders by Mack Ray Edwards? And what of Bob Jessup's encounter with just about the closest thing one can imagine to a real-life gargoyle? Devil's Gate Dam is not just a place that, for decades, has been filled with all-things negative, putrid, and hostile. It's also a place with a name that is just about as abominable as it is bleakly apt.

As much as you might prefer it, we are not yet done with the Devil. Leaving behind his deadly and cursed dam in California, it's time for us to sail his macabre, mysterious, and forever treacherous waters off the coast of Japan.

8

Devil's Sea, Japan

"On the other side of the world from the Bermuda Triangle there exists a section of the ocean startlingly similar in its history of vanishing ships and planes," stated Charles Berlitz, probably the one person who brought the infamous area's attention to the mainstream media and the general public. For the people of Japan, this treacherous and terror-soaked realm is one filled with notoriety. It is known as the Ma-no Umi: the Devil's Sea. Just like its far more famous cousin off the coast of Florida, this devilish body of water, which is near Miyake Island and approximately 62 miles south of Tokyo, can also claim to be responsible for hundreds of deaths and disappearances under very curious and disturbing circumstances. Also as with the Bermuda Triangle, the Devil's Sea is filled to the brim with sensational stories and tales of gateways to other worlds and dimensions; tales of dramatic alien encounters in the skies above the waters; and legends, folklore, and myths of great sea dragons that swallow ships whole and drag them to a dark underworld. And those stories are not just the stuff of the modern era. They date back a significant number of centuries (Berlitz, *The Bermuda Triangle*).

As a perfect and prime example, it is said that the legendary and powerful Mongolian warlord Kublai Khan attempted to flex his impressive muscles and might on Japan in the 1200s, but catastrophically failed to do so when his huge fleet of ships and their crews met their mysterious and deadly ends in the black heart of the Devil's Sea. On the first occasion, in 1274, a large number of ships and an untold number of men were lost to those hazardous waters. Seven years later, the picture was even worse. In a two-pronged attack, losses on the high seas from a military unit that had set sail from Masan, South Korea, amounted to 900 ships and 40,000 men of Mongol, Chinese, and Korean origin. And a gigantic fleet of 3,500 craft manned by 100,000 personnel fared even worse. Each and every one was utterly lost, and this was all before reaching the coastline and doing battle. The Devil's Sea was seemingly bent on ensuring that Kublai Khan's actions resulted in decimation, death, and disaster on repeated, gigantic scales.

It was these catastrophes that provoked a widespread belief that dragons had made this particular area of supernatural sea their home, and that these massive monsters had dragged the ships and their crews to the darkest depths of this eerie stretch of ocean. Could real-life dragons have actually reigned ruthlessly and majestically over the Devil's Sea in the distant past?

Richard Freeman, formerly a British zookeeper and an expert in dragon lore and mythology, makes a very intriguing observation on the admittedly highly controversial issue of whether at least some dragon legends might have a degree of basis in reality:

> Back in 1979 Peter Dickinson wrote a book that was titled *The Flight of Dragons*. Dickinson had come up with this idea—an excellent theory, in fact—that real-life dragons did exist and that they were the descendants of dinosaurs such as the Tyrannosaurus Rex. Dickinson suggested that these animals developed large, expanded stomachs that would fill with hydrogen gas, which would come from a combination of hydrochloric acid found in the juices of the digestive system that would then mix with calcium found in the bones of their prey.
>
> Then, from there, the hydrogen—a lighter-than-air gas—allowed these creatures to take to the skies and

then control their flight by burning off the excess gas in the form of flame. Anyone seeing this would be seeing the closest thing to the image of the dragon that we all know and love. Dickinson's theory is an excellent one, and may well be a perfect explanation for sightings of real dragons—in times past, and perhaps today, I believe.

The dragon has its teeth and claws deep into the collective psyche of mankind, and it's not about to let go. Our most ancient fear still stalks the earth today. Beware: this is no fairytale. When your parents told you that there were no such things as dragons, they lied! ("Enter the Dragon Hunter")

Legends tell of giant dragons prowling the Devil's Sea
(copyright Katsushika Hokusai)

Richard Freeman's undeniably captivating and thought-provoking revelations are made all the more remarkable by the experience of one Toksiakì Lang, a Japanese pilot who claimed that while flying over the Devil's Sea in 1944 and engaged in aerial combat with U.S. forces, he caught brief sight of an immense sea-serpent-type monster swimming the waters at high speed, with its long neck standing proudly and loftily as it did so. But, what makes Lang's story so notable is that he described the approximately 150-foot-long, dark-green-colored beast as possessing a pair of immense, triangular wings that seemed to help keep its mighty bulk afloat as it ploughed and stormed its way through the turbulent waters. A huge, serpent-like animal sporting two large, angled wings—a better description of a dragon would be very hard to ever capture. And wartime encounters with the unknown in the Devil's Sea continued during World War II. They were not all of a monstrous, dragon-based nature, however.

At the height of hostilities between the Allied and Axis powers, the Japanese military employed the use of Kawanishi HK-8 aircraft to search the skies for evidence of American military aircraft closing in on the mainland. And, in the event that such a penetration of Japanese borders might have occured, the crews were ready at a moment's notice to inform base headquarters of what was afoot. On one occasion, this resulted in a very strange and ultimately deadly message received at a military base on the Japanese mainland and on the doorstep of the Devil's Sea. The message was received by Shiro Kawamoto, who never forgot the chilling, confused, and final words of one of the panic-stricken crew members aboard the Kawanishi in question: "Something is happening to the sky...the sky is opening up" (Berlitz).

There the message abruptly, and forever, ended. Was it evidence of a cosmic kidnapping? Might the man have been describing a portal to another realm or dimension? To this day the case remains, like so many others, frustratingly unresolved.

The experience and story of Takeo Tada is undeniably one of the most significant on record when it comes to demonstrating that the Devil's Sea is a place of definitive paranormal proportions—and perhaps even of other-worldly proportions, too. On a pleasant but cloudy summer afternoon in 1971, Tada was flying adjacent to Miyake Island when he caught sight of something incredible that loomed out of the clouds only a half a mile or so from him. It was a flying saucer—an orange-colored, gleaming, circular-shaped craft of around 70 feet in diameter and 10 feet in height that traveled in a strange, wobbling fashion as it moved slowly through the sky.

Tada said that seeing the unusual aircraft momentarily, and hardly surprisingly, flummoxed him in the extreme, and he merely sat looking at it, astonished to his very core. After a minute or so, however, he regained his senses and chose to do something that some might view as brave and gung-ho and others as undeniably stupid and reckless: He gave chase. This was not a hard thing to do, even for Tada's small, propeller-driven aircraft. After all, he said, the UFO was traveling at barely 100 miles an hour, and the main challenge was not to keep up with it, but to avoid slamming into it! Fortunately, however, the plodding progress of the flying saucer ensured that Tada was able to get up close and personal, at which point he could see that it seemingly lacked windows, engines, wings, or a tail, and was sailing through the skies near Miyake Island in a magical, but laidback fashion. Tada continued to watch with both amazement and wonder until, after about nine or 10 minutes, the unearthly object slowly began to rise and travel in the direction of a large and dense cloud, into which it finally vanished, never to resurface. Tada, dumbstruck by the experience and fearful of what his colleagues and bosses might say or do if he dared tell them, chose—perhaps wisely—to remain silent on his unearthly encounter for more than 33 years.

Moving on to later years, in 1987, Tetsuzan Naito was flying his Cessna aircraft—just like Takeo Tada—near Miyake Island when, to his utter consternation and alarm and for 15 minutes, his on-board instrumentation and compass began to act in a distinctly haphazard fashion. Then, his engine repeatedly spluttered to the point where it seemed that at any given moment it might even catastrophically, and irreversibly, stall the plane, plunging Naito to a deadly end in the cold and clammy depths of the Devil's Sea. But, none of that compared to what happened at around seven or eight minutes into the highly fraught situation.

Without warning, and for no apparent reason that Naito could ever determine, his entire aircraft was suddenly engulfed in an eerie, green glow that appeared to extend to an all-encompassing distance of around 40 or 50 feet. Worse, Naito was suddenly hit by a severe bout of nausea and dizziness. Even more unsettling, an eerie, enveloping silence followed. The noise of the engine was gone, there appeared to be no wind outside, and even the sound of Naito frantically working the levers and instruments had been replaced by a complete lack of any noise at all. For all intents and purposes, Naito had been rendered deaf, or he had been plunged into a vacuum of paranormal proportions. That is until the instruments of Naito's Cessna suddenly righted themselves, noise levels returned to normal, and the sickly green glow vanished in an instant.

It's well worth noting that this green haze has also been reported in encounters emanating from the heart of the Bermuda Triangle. In November 1964, Chuck Wakeley was a pilot working for Miami, Florida-based Sunline Aviation. He recalled how, late on the night in question that all hell broke loose for him, he was en-route to Bimini, when he noticed a faint and mysterious glow on the wings of his aircraft. It was a haze that coincided with the electrical equipment of his aircraft going haywire, his fuel gauges giving conflicting readings, and his auto-pilot seemingly developing a chaotic life of its own—something that forced Wakeley to hastily turn it off and assume manual control of his aircraft. As for that haze, it was, Wakeley recalled, of a blue-green color. Fortunately, he came out of the incident unharmed, albeit distinctly perturbed, when the greenish haze faded away and normality soon returned in its wake.

Today, experienced pilots and mariners of the sea continue to report encounters of an irrational, enigmatic, and even supernatural nature in the Devil's Sea. And while the skeptics suggest flawed navigation, violent waters and equally violent skies, mechanical malfunction, and the rigors of Mother Nature can explain just about everything in a down-to-earth fashion, try telling that to those who have encountered the Devil Sea's dragons, UFOs, rifts in the skies, and aircraft-enveloping green fogs. They, I strongly suspect, will give you a very different, and highly alternative, set of answers to what may really be afoot in Satan's seas.

Still on the matter of things being afoot, in central England there exists a certain historic cemetery that is said to be the lair of a shape-shifting lycanthrope. Arm yourself with silver bullets. We're going on a werewolf hunt.

9

German Cemetery, Cannock Chase, England

A large forested plateau that borders the Trent Valley to the north and the West Midlands to the south, the huge and picturesque Cannock Chase has been a consistent feature of the Staffordshire, England, landscape for generations. Following an initial invasion of Britain in AD 43, Roman forces headed in a southerly direction to what is now the town of Cannock and along a major and historic Roman road now called Watling Street. The surrounding countryside was a widespread mass of forest even in those early times, as can be perfectly demonstrated by the Romans' name for the area: *Letocetum*, or, in modern terminology, the Grey Woods.

Designated officially by the British Government as an Area of Outstanding Beauty, the Chase runs to approximately 26 square miles of thick woodland and heath, is home to a huge herd of deer, and gained deep notoriety in the late 1960s when the remains of three young girls were found buried on the Chase. A Walsall, West Midlands, man named

Raymond Leslie Morris was found guilty of one of the killings—of 7-year-old Christine Darby—and was strongly suspected of having killed the other two: 6-year-old Margaret Reynolds, and Diana Joy Tift, who was just 5 years old. But outstanding beauty and terrible tragedy are not the only things that have shaped and sculpted the history of Cannock Chase. Throughout the years, the area has seemingly acted as a veritable magnet for all things supernatural, paranormal, and conspiratorial.

In 1991, a former U.S. Air Force intelligence officer named Leonard H. Stringfield revealed his knowledge of the crash of a UFO—an alien spacecraft, complete with a small crew of extraterrestrial entities—on the fringes of the Cannock Chase in early 1964, and which became the subject of a major cover-up on the part of British and NATO forces. The UFO, Stringfield said, had been tracked by the U.S. military moving in an irregular fashion high above Europe, before finally, and catastrophically, spiraling downward toward the Earth, fragmenting into several large pieces as it did so. A large portion of the UFO fell in a section of the Cannock Chase woods near the town of Penkridge, while a smaller piece apparently continued on its precarious journey and slammed into the ground somewhere along the East- and West-German border. Needless to say, the British Government denies any knowledge of this astonishing affair.

In the summer of 2003, strange rumors began to surface to the effect a fully grown crocodile was on the loose in Roman View Pond, a significantly sized body of water that borders the Cannock Chase. Despite apparent credible sightings of something large, monstrous, and green in color snaking through the dark waters, the mystery was never resolved and the beast vanished as quickly and as mysteriously as it had first appeared. Then, in 2005, sensational sightings were reported of a blazing-eyed, hulking, Bigfoot-type beast roaming the woods of the Castle Ring—an Iron Age structure commonly known as Hill Fort, which is located near the village of Cannock Wood, and which was constructed between 500 BC and AD 40 by a powerful tribe of warriors who held sway over the counties of Staffordshire, Cheshire, and Shropshire.

Although some cases demonstrate that the Cannock Chase, as a whole, is a place shrouded in supernatural strangeness, there is one particular location within those spooky woods that seems to just about outdo all of the others. It is a realm of the dead.

Located near Broadhurst Green, the German Cemetery is a memorial to more than 5,000 German servicemen who died within the British Isles during World War I and World War II, and whose graves are marked by headstones constructed out of Belgian granite and set in plots of heather. A tribute to the spirit of cooperation that now exists between the Commonwealth War Graves Commission and the Volksbund Deutsche Kriegsgraberfursorge (the German War Graves Commission), the cemetery had its origins in 1959, the year in which Germany made the initial approaches with a view to finding a site on the Chase near the existing Commonwealth Cemetery that contains the graves of 388 men from both wars, including 287 German soldiers.

In March 1962, the Staffordshire County Council made a gift of the land to the German Government, with the design of the cemetery and its surrounding buildings placed in the expert hands of Professor Diez Brandi of Gottingen, Germany, and Harold Doffman and Peter Leach, who, at the time, were partners in a Stafford firm of architects. As a result of the construction of the cemetery between 1964 and 1966, the bodies of numerous German servicemen, sailors buried at seaports around the British coast, airmen shot down inland, and soldiers—most of whom were prisoners-of-war buried in churchyards around the country—were transferred to the cemetery, which today can boast thousands of visitors per year, including some of a terrifying and tumultuous nature.

Since at least the late 1960s, sporadic reports have surfaced from pretty much the entirety of the Cannock Chase of large and marauding black cats that, collectively, have become known as the *Chase Panther*. Between 1996 and 2000, however, such sightings reached epidemic proportions in the direct vicinity of the German Cemetery. In one case, the witness described a startling encounter that suggested the creature may have had definitive paranormal origins. Eileen Allen says that she caught sight of what she described as a very large black cat while visiting the cemetery in the latter part of 1996. The utter shock of seeing the immense beast lurking near one of the headstones, and staring intently in Allen's direction, was nothing compared to the absolute terror that struck her when it suddenly vanished into thin air amid a sound that Allen described as static electricity. Not surprisingly, Allen fled the cemetery and has never returned to the scene of the anomalous action.

Robert and Jean Beeston were among those who encountered big cat activity at the cemetery, too. In their case, which occurred in 2000, although they only had the creature in their sights for mere moments as they drove past the graves, Robert Beeston was absolutely certain of what he and his wife both saw: "It was a big, black panther. It was massive; with one leap it cleared the road. We weren't afraid; it was just an incredible sight" ("Chase Beast").

In June 2001, Mike Johnson, who was heavily involved in surveying vegetation on the Cannock Chase for the University and the Stafford-shire Wildlife Trust, was walking the woods slightly due north of the German Cemetery when something highly strange occurred, something that still troubles and perplexes him to this very day. It was around 2 p.m. on a clear, sunny day and Johnson was searching for examples of the Midland Hawthorn. All was well until, quite out of the blue, an eerie and all-encompassing silence overwhelmed the area. But there was something even more worrying: Johnson suddenly found himself severely disoriented; as Johnson told it, the landscape seemed curiously unfamiliar. The path he had traveled from the cemetery was now on his west, when it should have been on his east. The early afternoon sun even seemed to be in the wrong place. Johnson was barely any distance at all from the German Cemetery, a place he knew very well, but for all intents and purposes, he was completely lost of all bearings. Then something occurred that was as terrifying as it was amazing.

Some distance away, and while still feeling seriously confused, Johnson could see a curious character. It appeared to be a tall man with very thin arms and legs, and who, at first glance, Johnson assumed was dressed entirely in gray. But, as Johnson looked closer, and more intently, he could see there was something very wrong about the man. He wasn't just tall, but *very* tall. His head was hairless and elongated to a very significant degree. His neck was spindly. And, most noticeable of all, his arms seemed to reach past his knees. This was no mere hiker or someone looking for a place to have a picnic. Johnson had been plunged into the depths of some bizarre nightmare—except he was wide awake.

Eventually, and fortunately, the eerie silence gave way to the familiar sounds of the woods and the landscape, such as the chirping of birds and the chattering of ramblers. The disorientation and the sense of being lost faded away, as did the strange, gray giant. And just like Eileen Allen, who encountered a big cat at the German Cemetery in 1996, Mike Johnson still has yet to the return to the site of the surreal weirdness he encountered in the summer of 2001.

It's worth noting that the phenomenon of disorientation Mike Johnson described is nothing new. His strange experience at the German Cemetery on the Cannock Chase brings to mind the words of Margaret Ann Courtney, a noted expert in English folklore, and particularly that of the county of Cornwall.

In 1890, she said of the games and manipulative behavior of fairies, goblins, and a wide assortment of what have become collectively known as the "little people" or the "wee folk" that: "When mischievously inclined pisky often leads benighted people a sad dance; like Will of the Wisp, he takes them over hedges and ditches, and sometimes round and round the same field, from which they in vain try to find their way home, although they can always see the path close at hand" (Courtney).

The werewolf-infested German Cemetery of England's Cannock Chase (copyright Nick Redfern)

Mysterious black cats and the deeply strange affair of Mike Johnson were nothing compared to the putrid thing that briefly haunted the German Cemetery in 2007, however. If the terrified and terrorized witnesses were not mistaken, a nightmarish werewolf had descended upon the sacred ground. It was a creature that struck deep fear into the hearts of those who dwelled in the little hamlets that populate the Cannock Chase. It even had some of them refusing to leave their homes after the sun had set, and particularly so on nights blessed—if that is the correct word to use—by a full moon.

It all began in April 2007, when a local, well respected group of paranormal investigators, the *West Midlands Ghost Club*, traveled out to the area to investigate newly surfaced reports of what witnesses described as a large, hairy creature very much resembling a wolf. But, there was something extremely weird about this particular wolf: as well as walking like any normal wolf might, this one had the amazing and uncanny ability to rear up onto its hind limbs, which it invariably did when anyone had the distinct misfortune to cross its malevolent path.

One of those whose encounter caught the attention of one of the club's investigators, Nick Duffy, was a mailman who was riding past the cemetery on a motorbike when he became spellbound by the sight of what, at first, he assumed was a large, wild wolf on the loose. This would be extraordinary enough in itself, as the wild wolf is generally acknowledged as having become extinct in the British Isles centuries ago. That the creature was no mere normal wolf, however, became very obvious to the shocked man when it caught his eye, raised itself upwards on its back legs, and bounded away into the countless trees that envelop the cemetery.

The next witness to come forward to Nick Duffy and his colleagues was a local scout-leader who was walking around the cemetery when he experienced something similar. Quite understandably not wanting to speak out on the record, Duffy's source, too, initially assumed that the creature he saw lurking among the graves was a wolf—or possibly even a large dog, such as a Husky. It was neither. On realizing that the animal was seemingly running wild, the man slowly and carefully retreated to the safety of his car and slammed the door, at which point, on hearing the noise, the beast rose up on its back legs to an incredible height of

7 feet, and raced off into the heart of the woods. The shocking encounter was over. The controversy, however, was just getting started.

The local newspaper, the *Chase Post*, soon got in on the action and began publishing reports suggesting the werewolf secretly made its lair deep amid the many natural caverns and winding, old, man-made mines and shafts that exist deep below the surface of the Cannock Chase. The beast, some speculated, possibly had a point of entrance and exit somewhere close to the cemetery—something which hardly generated much cheer in those that lived nearby. And that the sightings of the monstrous thing coincided with the mysterious disappearance of a sizeable number of pet dogs in the area, and that several deer had been found horribly mutilated and with significant organs torn out and flesh viciously removed too, only served to increase the escalating anxiety about the presence of the monster of the cemetery.

As the sightings of the werewolf continued, and the dog disappearances duly escalated, so did the controversy. Derek Crawley, the chairman of the *Staffordshire Mammal Society*, expressed his view that although a wolf could, in theory at least, make a home for itself on the Cannock Chase, in this case there were a couple of problems. First, there was the fact that wolves should not have been running wild anywhere in Britain during the first decade of the 21st century. Plus, as Crawley also noted, wolves are pack animals. But, the werewolf of the German Cemetery seemed to be an overwhelmingly solitary beast. No one walking around the graves had ever seen more than one on any given occasion. Crawley did note, quite correctly, that there were a number of local people who owned Huskies, and he opined that this may have been what people were seeing. Indeed, such a theory might have been considered not just a possibility, but a downright probability, had it not been for that troubling issue of the beast seen running on two legs as well as four. Thus, with the witnesses steadfastly standing by their claims and assertions, the mystery remained. Or, it's correct to say it remained until the late summer of 2007, when the werewolf (if that is what it really was) vanished either into the ether, some dark and mysterious realm of paranormal origins, or those shadowy tunnels beneath the old woods.

But, as the mystery came to its end, a very weird observation was made. One of those buried in the German Cemetery is a man named

Maximilian von Herff. Born on April 17, 1893, von Herff served as an officer with Germany's Reichswehr in World War I, attained the rank of colonel, and went on to win the Iron Cross. During World War II, von Herff served in North Africa as commander of the Kampfgruppe and went on to join Hitler's notorious and much-feared SS. He died in 1945 in Britain's Conishead Priory Military Hospital, having previously been held at the nearby Grizedale Prisoner of War Camp.

It turns out that Nazi Germany had established a clandestine resistance force that would undertake guerrilla-style attacks against the Allies in the event that the Nazi regime came to an end. The group was approximately 5,000 in number and was comprised of members of the SS and the Hitler Youth, including von Herff. Its nickname was the *Werewolves*. So, in a very roundabout and highly strange way, there really *were* werewolves at the German Cemetery—most certainly Nazi ones, and very possibly a most savage and monstrous one.

Savage and monstrous are also most apt descriptions for more than a few of the horrific things that roam the wilds of our next port of call. It's a place as mysterious as it is magical.

10

Guadalcanal, Solomon Islands, Oceania

Named by Alvaro de Mendana, a noted Spanish explorer who, in 1568, became the very first European to visit them, the Solomon Islands are to be found east of Papua New Guinea. They number almost 1,000 in total, and can claim a history that dates back many thousands of years. Proof of the presence of man in the islands has been traced to approximately 30,000 BC. And, there is strong evidence to show that the native population was, for a considerable period of time at least, distinctly savage and brutal in nature. Both head-hunting and cannibalism were rife before the islanders fell under the sway of Christianity and the Europeans who followed in the wake of de Mendana's 16th-century arrival. Bringing matters far more up to date, the Solomon Islands played a key and decisive role in World War II: They were the site of the famous Battle of Guadalcanal between American and Japanese forces that extended from August 1942 to February 1943.

And it is Guadalcanal, the largest of all the Solomon Islands, that is populated by some seriously strange things of a wildly varying nature.

Named after Guadalcanal, Spain—which happened to be the birthplace of a man named Pedro de Ortega Valencia, a member of Alvaro de Mendana's 1568 expedition—the island has an extensive history of encounters with enormous creatures for which the word *giant* might have been justifiably created. Back in the 1940s, as the Guadalcanal conflict was about to erupt—and close to where, today, the rotted hulls of wartime ships still lie, steadily crumbling more and more, year by year—a large, circular-shaped UFO briefly dominated the skyline and set U.S. military forces on full-alert status. And tales of massive creatures that resemble, but that easily dwarf in size, the legendary Abominable Snowmen of the Himalayas and the North American Bigfoot are deeply rooted in the culture and lore of the islanders. But before we get to those, we'll start with something very different: the Solomon Islands' very own dragons.

A staple part of the folklore of the people is a legendary, monster serpent; it's a winged fire-breather known as the Hatuibwari or, alternately, as Agunua. And it's an undeniably fearsome beast to behold. Though its body is definitively snake-like in appearance, texture, and color, its head and face are utterly human—aside, that is, from the extra pair of wildly staring eyes that sit square in its forehead. Add to that four breasts, vicious claws on each hand, and a huge pair of bat-like wings that protrude from its scaly spine, and we have what sounds like an unholy and bizarre nightmare of the type that so obsessed H.P. Lovecraft. But we would be very wrong. Sometimes the old adage that appearances can be deceiving is absolutely right on target. The Hatuibwari is actually a deeply revered and respected entity of supernatural origins, one that in the culture of the people of the Solomon Islands is believed to have been the creator of all things and the giver, and caretaker, of life. The legendary beast is also perceived as a full-fledged deity, one that rules over the seas of the Solomon Islands, as well as the land and all its people.

The folk of Guadalcanal have intriguing, longstanding beliefs about the mysteries surrounding life after death, too. The stories demonstrate a solid, longstanding acceptance that the human soul has duality: after death, one part of it is destined either for a magical island or a dark realm located deep underground, whereas the other aspect of the human essence reincarnates in the form of an animal of the land, sea, or skies.

Even to this very day, in those particular areas of the Solomon Islands where the practices of old still continue unabated and Christianity does not dominate, the head of a recently deceased person may be floated into the sea by the family; then, whichever creature of the oceans first approaches the head will signify to the mourners the particular form in which the person's soul is destined to reincarnate in its next existence.

Shape-shifting, man-eating monsters of a distinctly ogre-like variety are highly prevalent in the folklore and legends of the Solomon Islands, too. Human beings, crocodiles, and pigs are just some of the preferred forms into which these particularly savage creatures manifest as they seek to deceive, and ultimately devour, the innocent and unwary. Although these latter stories of giants sound far more like the stuff of folklore than reality, rather incredibly they may actually have a solid basis in fact—albeit somewhat heavily distorted fact.

Marius Boirayon, who lived and worked in the Solomon Islands as a helicopter pilot and engineer, and who has extensively researched the tales of the area's resident giants, has uncovered an extraordinary body of data on the controversy that strongly negates the idea that they are just the stuff of wild legend. Notably, many of the accounts suggest the renowned tales of the giants may have their origins in the Solomon Islands' very own equivalent of Bigfoot. Boirayon has, for example, investigated countless reports of huge, fierce-looking, humanoid creatures—in excess of a mighty10 feet in height—that are covered in coats of long, dark brown and sometimes reddish hair, and that possess flat noses, wide mouths, and bulging red eyes; all of which are typical of the descriptions of the Sasquatch of the Pacific northwest.

Incredibly, there appears to be not just one type of such creature in the Solomon Islands, but *three*: The first is a truly huge creature that reportedly can reach stratospheric heights of 15 to 20 feet, a second that still towers over the average human at a somewhat more modest 10 feet, and a smaller, less hairy variety that is described as being more like a wild man than a wild ape. And each and every one of them is quite partial to tasty human women, too. And I don't mean for food.

Marius Boirayon uncovered the deeply disturbing story of a woman named Mango, who, decades ago, was said to have been ruthlessly kidnapped by one of the hairy goliaths and taken to its dark den, which was situated deep in the wilds of Guadalcanal. For an astonishing 25 years, and before her final, successful escape from the monstrous clutches, Mango was forced to endure a nightmarish existence among the beasts and even bore a hideous-looking child to one of them—surely a good indication that, if the story is true, the creatures are of a proto-human variety, rather than being specifically ape-like. Not surprisingly, the years-long experience had rendered Mango utterly mad as a hatter. A very cautionary and tragic tale.

How do such extraordinarily large man-monsters so successfully hide from just about one and all? Though dense, tropical jungle absolutely abounds throughout Guadalcanal, one would imagine that evidence of the huge lairs of the beasts would be stumbled upon at least once, and the shocking truth would then tumble out. But it seems researchers have been searching in all of the wrong places: They have been looking around in the woods, when, instead, they really should have been looking below them into the heart of the island's cavernous underworld. Certainly, the people of Guadalcanal have sensational stories of vast cave systems that wind their way throughout, and under, the mountains of the island and in which, it is quietly whispered, the hairy giants live, and in numbers that are now said to possibly reach the thousands.

According to local mythology, one such entrance points to what has been described as a vast underground city of monsters can be found on Mount Tattiva, should you have the urge to try and find your way into this hellish realm. And lest you think all of these stories are nothing more than oral tradition, distorted and added to throughout generations by unnamed souls, they are certainly not. Ezekiel Alebua, who just happens to have been the third Prime Minister of the Solomon Islands—from December 1986 to March 1989—has stated that as a child, and in the company of his father, he was taken to a cave in the eastern part of the island, where, to his amazement, he was shown the remains of a vast, 15-foot-tall, humanoid skeleton. But, it's not just from Guadalcanal that traditions of giants roaming the Solomon Islands emanate. Santa Isabel Island, the island of Choiseul, and Malaita all have similar tales of massive, hairy humanoids attached to them. From the leader of the Solomon Islands down, and from isle to isle, the gargantuan man-beasts of the jungles are as widely known and accepted as being real, feared, and avoided at all costs.

Aliens, giants, and Bigfoot all call Guadalcanal their home
(copyright U.S. Navy)

Two days before the battle of Guadalcanal began, a spectacular
UFO encounter occurred that involved numerous U.S. military personnel who were all geared up to take on the Japanese. On the day in
question, all was unsurprisingly tense among the American personnel
aboard the *USS Helm* that was due to play a major role in the looming
face-off with the Japanese. But, it was not only the Axis powers that
the ship's crew had to worry about. Around 10 a.m., the radar operators
of another vessel reported to the *USS Helm* that they were tracking the
movements of an unidentified object rapidly closing in on the American
fleet, which quickly went to full-alert status; but this was no normal
Japanese fighter-plane in a surprise attack. Traveling at a tremendous
speed that the gunners aboard the *USS Helm* could not even begin to
keep up with—and which, at one point, was estimated to be flying in the
range of thousands, rather than hundreds, of miles per hour—the UFO
performed astonishingly tight right- and left-hand turns as it circled the

flotilla of warships, and ran rings around the astonished sailors who were struggling just to see the blurry, racing thing in the sky, never mind bring it down.

One of the crew members finally caught sight of it. Armed with a pair of powerful binoculars, he was able to see, at a height of around 3,000 feet, a circular-shaped, fairly flat, silver-colored object that was clearly unlike anything the Americans, British, Germans, or Japanese were flying at the time. And although the term *flying saucer* would not be coined for another five years, for all intents and purposes, that is exactly what was maneuvering over the fleet. Or, it was until, displaying a near-unbelievable rate of acceleration, it shot away, never to return. Despite intensive investigations by Command Headquarters, the UFO remained unidentified and the event was quietly filed away in a definitively unexplained category.

Numerous gigantic Bigfoot, legendary dragons as deities, human-devouring ogres, wartime flying saucers, and a strange, soul-splitting afterlife where people reincarnate in the form of animals: welcome to the supernatural world and inhabitants of Guadalcanal.

Equally supernatural, but for reasons vastly different, is an old and charming locale in Nova Scotia, Canada, where the restless dead are so many in number they overwhelm the living.

11

Halifax, Nova Scotia, Canada

The origins of Halifax, Nova Scotia, date back to May 14, 1749, when Edward Cornwallis, a Lieutenant with the British Army, set sail from England aboard the HMS *Sphinx*. The purpose was to develop a significantly sized British settlement in Canada that would be a viable counter to France's powerful and strategically significant Fortress of Louisburg. Along with Cornwallis were more than 2,500 settlers and 15 ships, all ready for the impressive and ambitious task at-hand. On June 21st, the fleet arrived and development duly began. It was hardly a peaceful time, however. Outraged First Nations Micmac people launched deadly attacks on the British for what they saw as flagrant disregard of an earlier treaty guaranteeing peace and, worse still, as outright theft of Micmac land. The so-called Seven Years' War of 1756 to 1763, in which the Micmac tribe was allied with the French, added to the large-scale turbulence and death, until victory came to Britain and Halifax began to develop and thrive. Today, Halifax is a busy municipality with a population of more than 400,000, and a place that, as well as very much keeping up with the times, has successfully retained its old-world charm, its rich history, and its captivating architecture that hark back to a time long-past. And, lest I forget: Halifax is weird.

For years, sea serpents have purportedly loomed large in the waters of Halifax. The afternoon of July 15, 1825, turned out to be a most memorable one for an amazed group that included William Barry and Mr. Goreham and his family and servants—all of whom were in the harbor area of Halifax when from the waters surfaced…*something*. They were all clear on, and deeply shocked by, the nature of the mysterious creature briefly in their midst. Snake-like, it was around 60 feet in length, and propelled itself along the waters in an odd and curiously unsettling wiggling motion.

Then, on May 16, 1833, the crew of a British naval vessel had a close encounter of the monstrous and serpentine variety near Halifax's St. Margaret's Bay and Mahone Bay. One of those aboard the ship, Henry Ince, said of the crew's remarkable experience:

> At the distance of from 150 to 200 yards on our starboard bow we saw the head and neck of some denizen of the deep, precisely like those of a common snake, in the act of swimming, the head so far elevated and thrown forward by the curve of the neck as to enable us to see the water under and beyond it. We were of course all taken aback at the sight, and with staring eyes and in speechless wonder stood gazing at it for full half a minute: there could be no mistake, no delusion, and we were all perfectly satisfied that we had been favored with a view of the "true and veritable sea serpent." ("Halifax Sea Serpent")

Two decades later, just such a beast was back yet again.

Early one morning in August 1853, a man named Peter McNab, Jr. caught sight of a true serpent of the seas off Ives Point, which provides a panoramic and captivating view of Halifax's spacious harbor. In McNab's very own words: "At [6:30] this morning, when returning from McNab's Island I saw a Sea Serpent over 20 feet long, between the Red Buoy, and the NW point of the island moving very rapidly. It greatly resembled a large eel—had a very small head raised 2 or 3 inches above the water, and it moved in an undulating motion" (PSICAN Group).

It's worth noting that 20 years later, McNab wound up in Mount Hope Asylum (today the Nova Scotia Hospital), having gone utterly insane and found guilty of grievous bodily harm (the details of which are unknown). He died there shortly after his incarceration. One hopes it was not the enduring, horrific memory of the monster of the deep that provoked McNab's madness and death. Now, with sea serpents and insanity behind us: on to Halifax's UFOs.

Shortly before the witching hour on the night of October 27, 1976, Constable P. Pharand, of the Royal Canadian Mounted Police, received a fascinating report from the Sackville area of Halifax of unusual, and maybe even unearthly, phenomena in the heavens. Having listened carefully to the words of the witnesses—Mr. and Mrs. Percy Webster— Pharand wasted no time in jumping in his patrol vehicle and heading out to the scene of the action. It was a very wise move. There was something extremely weird going on in the mysterious darkness above, as Pharand later noted in his official report on the anomalous affair:

> …upon arrival and with the aid of the complainants' bin-oculars I noticed three unidentified flying objects. All of them were round in shape and had red flashing lights on the bottom and also a flashing white light. There was a stable green light which appeared to be located inside the objects. At this time the objects were stationary; however, I noticed that they began to move and when they did, the lights changed to a turquoise color. As the objects began to move, their altitude became greater. (Pharand, 1976)

Might the objects actually have been helicopters or airplanes? Not according to staff at the Halifax International Airport, who made careful and speedy checks and came up totally blank. Notably, the staff even offered that they were seeing nothing on radar, either. So, what was it that the Websters and Pharand were watching? The officer was adamant that regardless of what they were, he knew for sure they were not stars or planets. So, with both aircraft and astronomical phenomena now ruled out, the curious objects were practically destined to become UFOs. Consciously or not, Pharand himself appeared to have to come to this conclusion himself, because his report was specifically titled *UNIDEN-TIFIED FLYING OBJECTS, Sightings of—Lower Sackville*.

There is one curious afterword to this story: Pharand's report referred to other witnesses—Mr. and Mrs. Robert Bedford. In 1996, a Halifax-based UFO researcher, Chris Styles, managed to track down the pair and engaged them in conversation about the encounter. Interestingly, both denied having seen anything strange in the skies that night, despite what had been written about them in the Royal Canadian Mounted Police report. The reason: At the time, they were hiding in the upstairs section of their home with the blinds drawn, as a loud and persistent roar overwhelmed the house. Although they didn't see it, something strange, they were sure, was hovering above it. As for the noise, Mr. Bedford said it was certainly not of the sort one would normally associate with a helicopter or aircraft. Bedford was careful to stress that, as a naval architect, he was very familiar with both. And, that the Bedford's were barricaded in their home, and practically overwhelmed by the thunderous noise, at the exact same time Constable Pharand and the Websters were seeing unknown objects that lacked any sound whatsoever, only made matters even more bizarre. But, when it comes to the mystery of UFOs, should we really expect anything less than outright bizarreness? Unidentified flying objects, and gigantic serpents of the deep, pale in comparison when it comes to Halifax's legion of resident ghosts, however.

In the wake of a cataclysmic explosion in its harbor in 1917, Halifax, Nova Scotia's dead rose from the grave (copyright Wikimedia Commons, 1917)

On the fatal and fateful morning of December 6, 1917, Halifax's harbor became the scene of deep tragedy and massive death when two ships, the French Freighter, *Mont Blanc* and the *Imo*, a whaling supply ship, catastrophically collided. Fire rapidly broke out aboard the *Mont Blanc*, and given that its cargo included a significant amount of TNT that was destined for then-war-torn Europe, the crew literally jumped ship. Shortly after 9 a.m., and with the fire by now raging wildly out of control, there was a massive explosion. The *Mont Blanc* was vaporized, approximately 2,000 people were killed, more than double that number were injured, and more than 1,500 buildings in Halifax were flattened. And in the wake of the complete and utter disaster, ghosts and specters loomed large—and they still do so today, almost a century later.

One of those that legend says was killed as a result of the pulverizing blast was a woman who has become a spooky fixture of Halifax: the Gray Nun, who haunts the Victoria General Hospital. She is no maniacal and macabre monster intent on scaring the life out of those she encounters, however. The woman in gray is a kindly soul who appears to possess the uncanny skill of knowing when death is about to close in on those patients destined never to leave the hospital. She hovers around them, offering comfort and guidance as the end grows nearer. And how is her presence most often detected? By the slight, yet always noticeable fragrance of incense that forever accompanies the Gray Nun on her wanderings.

Then there is the reputedly haunted St. Paul's Anglican Church, which is located on Argyle Street, on Halifax's Grand Parade. Or, it may be more correct to say that it's not the church itself that is said to be haunted, but one of its windows! Despite having been replaced on a number of occasions, the pane of glass in question consistently appears to show the silhouette of a man's head and shoulders. If not the ongoing work of a prankster secretly intent on carving a silhouette-style image every time the glass is changed, it may represent one of several people, depending on who you care to ask. Some say it appears to resemble Reverend Jean-Baptiste Moreau, an assistant at the church in the mid-1800s. Others say the image was provoked by the death of a young organist, who was violently decapitated when the cargo of the *Mont Blanc* exploded on December 6, 1917. But, whatever its

origin—ghost or on-going joker—the spectral head of glass is a real—
ahem—head-turner.

Also on Argyle Street—at 1740, directly across the street from St.
Paul's Anglican Church, to be precise—is the Five Fishermen, a very
popular and atmospheric seafood restaurant with far more than a few
ghostly goings-on attached to it. Opened in 1816, originally as a Church
of England National School, it later became the Halifax Victorian School
of Art which happened to be run by Anna Leonowens—the very same
Anna of the classic book, *Anna and the King of Siam* and the musical,
The King and I. But, it was after 1974 when the old building became the
Five Fishermen, that the strangeness began in full force.

The proprietors and staff of the restaurant have eagerly embraced
the paranormal activity among them and are more than willing to share
the supernatural experiences with anyone who cares to listen. And that's
good, because there's plenty to talk about. Faucets turn themselves on
and off. Apparitional figures have been seen near the swing-doors leading to the kitchen. A mist-like mass of cloud haunts the grand stairwell
that takes one to the maître d stand. There is the old man who appears
now and again in a period-costume and long, dark coat befitting centuries long-past. Whispered, disembodied voices strike fear and anxiety in
those who hear them. And sudden drops in temperature—to what feel
like near-freezing levels—are commonplace. But, why should the Five
Fishermen be such a hive of horror and weirdness?

After Anna Leonowens left, the building became the John Snow
and Co. Funeral Home, and when the disaster of December 6, 1917
occurred, many of the bodies of those killed by the blast were taken to
the building, first for storage and, as soon as was conceivably possible,
burial. Indeed, nearly a full century later, stories still circulate of the
dozens and dozens of coffins piled up outside the Five Fishermen as the
people of Halifax struggled to cope with the unimaginable scale of the
tragedy that devastatingly hit them. So, it's hardly surprising that with
so much death and mayhem in residence, the dead continue to hover
around the place. But, some suggest, many of the ghosts of the restaurant may have far less to do with the explosion of the *Mont Blanc*, and
far more to do with an even more infamous sea-based tragedy, one of
titanic proportions.

April 15, 1912 is the date of one of the worst events in maritime history: the sinking of the British-built RMS *Titanic*, after its collision with an iceberg 375 miles south of Newfoundland, on its maiden voyage from Southampton, England, to New York. Given the location of the disaster, a number of Canadian ships, boats, and their crews played significant roles in the recovery of the bodies of the *Titanic*, which amounted to 1,514 passengers and crew. One of those ships, the *Mackay-Bennett*, happened to be based out of Halifax.

The sheer number of bodies in question was of such a scale that recovering and embalming all of them for the journey to Halifax was clearly impossible; and so only the bodies of first-class passengers were saved, while the huge remainder was given burials at sea. Many of those corpses that were preserved, however, made their way for storage to the Five Fishermen. Or, as it was known at the time: the John Snow and Co. Funeral Home. From there, the bodies were given respectful burials in Halifax's Fairview Lawn, Baron de Hirsch, and Mount Olivet cemeteries. So, we have yet another disaster of immense proportions and massive loss of life inextricably linked to the infamous restaurant. And, hardly surprisingly, given what we know of its historic past and its resident spirits, the Five Fishermen is a place that has attracted the careful attention of the local media.

Paul Kimball is a highly regarded Halifax-based filmmaker who has spent a great deal of time researching the ghosts of his hometown, including those of the Five Fishermen. In 2009, for his show *Ghost Cases*, Kimball and his co-host, Holly Stevens, spent significant hours at the restaurant speaking with the staff about their eerie and extraordinary experiences. Leonard Currie told the paranormal sleuths that he had a number of strange encounters, but added that the oddest one occurred shortly after he began working at the Five Fishermen. It was mid-afternoon and Currie was setting up the salad bar when he suddenly heard a crash from behind him. An ashtray had fallen to the ground, which Currie admitted he found somewhat unusual, but didn't give it that much thought and just bent down to pick it up. Having done so, he noticed something decidedly odd: In an adjacent mirror, he could see the figure of a man. This was no customer, however. Rather, it was a character dressed in the clothes of a long-gone era. In an instant, it was gone.

For a long time, and hardly surprisingly, Currie told no one of his curious experience.

The ghosts of the Five Fishermen, it seems very safe to say, live on and are likely to continue doing so. Disaster and death on the high seas, the long-dead still lingering around town, mega-sized monsters surfacing from deep under the waves, and UFOs manifesting from the skies: just a bit of everyday life, albeit very weird everyday life, in Halifax, Nova Scotia.

And now, to quote a certain hit song, welcome to the jungle.

12

Han River, Vietnam

It was a calm and muggy summer's night, only four months before the dawning of the 1970s, and Earl Morrison, who was a private in the U.S. Marine Corps, was stationed in Vietnam, sitting and chatting with two friends atop a bunker situated near Da Nang, a port city on the coast of the South China Sea, at the mouth of the Han River. For reasons that Morrison and his friends were never really able to make clear sense of, they all simultaneously turned their attentions skyward, and, to their total astonishment and unmitigated horror, saw a strange and terrifying figure crossing the vast expanse of the evening sky. And, worse still, it was slowly coming right toward them: "We saw what looked like wings, like a bat's; only it was gigantic compared to what a regular bat would be. After it got close enough so we could see what it was, it looked like a woman, a naked woman" (Worley).

The winged woman, added Morrison, was entirely jet-black in color, but seemed to have a greenish glow about her, too. As she closed in on the dumbstruck trio, and duly passed over them at a height of barely

6 feet, they could hear the distinct flapping of powerful wings. Too astonished to do anything but sit in silence and awe, Morrison and his comrades simply stared for three or four minutes until the flying woman finally sailed away and vanished into the growing darkness of the Vietnamese skies. A strange, flying bat-woman is not the only thing to haunt the Han River, however. A gigantic Loch Ness Monster-type serpent is said to dwell deep within the magical waters of the large river. And, ghostly balls of floating light roam the river and its immediate surroundings.

Even the most cursory study of worldwide folklore reveals that numerous, if not all, cultures have stories attached to them of magical balls of floating light, seemingly under intelligent control, or perhaps even supernatural, sentient forms of life in their very own right. They travel the skies by night, while amazing, perplexing, and sometimes even terrifying those who encounter them, very often in the vicinity of marshes, bogs, and other watery bodies. The specific, repeated locations of many such sightings has given rise to the not unreasonable notion that at least some of the lights may be nothing stranger than the results of methane bubbling up out of the marshes and mixing with phospine, a flammable gas, and an inorganic compound called diphosphane, which, when combined with the air, can briefly and spontaneously catch fire in spectacular fashion.

Others suggest the culprit may be a rare phenomenon known as ball lightning. A technical report published in 1949 by the Air Force's UFO investigative unit, *Project Grudge*, detailed its findings with respect to ball lightning which, the military believed, was connected to regular lightning and electrical discharge. The phenomenon, it was noted, was "spherical, roughly globular, egg-shaped, or pear-shaped; many times with projecting streamers; or flame-like irregular 'masses of light.' Luminous in appearance, described in individual cases by different colors but mostly reported as deep red and often as glaring white." Thus, the ghostly lights, and their attendant legends, are well and truly born. These two particular down-to-earth theories have not, in any shape or fashion, dispelled the belief that the majority of such lights have far weirder origins, however (*Unidentified Flying Objects*).

A classic example of a ghostly ball of light similar to that seen at the Han River (copyright Wikimedia Commons, 19th century)

England, for example, has its very own squadron of ghostly lights. Depending on the particular region of the country that you care to examine, they go by the ancient names of the Pixy Light, Will o' the Wisp, and Rolling Fire. The people of Wales have their own equivalent: It is known as Fairy Fire. The Chir Batti is an identical entity that haunts the land in and around the India-Pakistan border. Bengal is the domain of the glowing and flying Aleya. Brazil can claim the Boi-tata. Throughout much of eastern Australia, tales are told of the Min Min Light. The Naga Fireballs are a regular phenomenon along the length of Thailand's Mekong River. And in the United States, one can find entertaining stories of the Marfa Lights of Texas, and the Brown Mountain Light of North Carolina, among numerous others.

Many of these legends, despite originating among wildly varying cultures and countries, and across numerous centuries, have one notable thing in common: the mysterious lights are believed to be the tormented souls of people who committed heinous crimes in life, or were the victims of deep tragedy and/or suicide, and are destined never to rest in peace and harmony. And that goes, too, for the Han River's very own ghost light, the Nayaga, the name of which may quite possibly be a derivation of the Thai Naga.

The Nayaga is said to be the ethereal form of a rich nobleman who held sway over much of the area from the late 18th century to the early 19th century. Furious at his teenage daughter's relationship with a poor, young blacksmith in a small, poor village on the river itself, the man, ordered one of his servants to secretly follow the girl's lover to his place of work and spike his supply of drinking water with a deadly, fast-acting poison, which the servant dutifully and appropriately cold of heart, did. The servant then found a shadowy place to hide in the nearby bushes and kept a careful watch on the boy; patiently and eagerly awaiting the moment when thirst from working under the hot, morning sun guaranteed the blacksmith would take a large gulp of water and death would soon overtake him. But fate and disaster intervened in a catastrophic way that none could ever have foreseen.

Suddenly, and to the horror of the servant, the nobleman's daughter appeared on the scene—having slipped out of the spacious abode in which she lived with her father. She flung her arms tightly around her boyfriend, gave him a loving kiss, and then, dehydrated from her long walk along the riverbank, took a big swig of water from the poisoned container. In just mere moments, she collapsed to the floor, proclaiming her eternal love to the devastated young blacksmith as she took her very last breaths.

The servant raced out of the trees to try to help, but it was all too late. Death already had the girl in its grip. And it soon came to call upon her father, too. On hearing the tragic news, the distraught old man flung himself from the highest balcony of his palace, ensuring his violent and bloody death on the stone pavement below. But, he soon returned. Not, however, as a chain-rattling, moaning specter, but in the form of a glowing ball of light forever fated to wander the skies of the Han River by night. Out of love and death, the Nayaga was born. And if you should ever visit the area and you are lucky enough to see the ghostly phenomenon for yourself, spare a deep thought or several for all those whose lives were snuffed out, or forever scarred, by this harrowing series of events. It must be said that a story like this might simply have been a story and nothing more. But, even if that is so, a strong argument can still be made that the tale was created to explain the presence of a very real and perplexing phenomenon of the Han River: the Nayaga light.

In July 2009, construction of a truly massive bridge over the Han River began. With a planned overall length of more than 2,200 feet and a width of 123 feet, it will, when finally completed in late 2012 or early 2013, comprise of six lanes to allow for extensive traffic to flow to and from the city of Da Nang and its growing, international airport. Its name is to be the Dragon River Bridge, and it will even be fashioned in the shape of one of the legendary, fire-breathing reptilians of ancient mythology. The name of the bridge is certainly a most apt one, because the water of the Han River is the domain of a Vietnamese equivalent of Scotland's Loch Ness Monster.

Admittedly, sightings of the creature of the river are scarce, but they do exist. And, they span a number of years, too, thus making the possibility that the beast is a real one—rather than one of mythological proportions—all the more likely. Both cases, rather surprisingly, come not from the files of respected monster-hunters and cryptozoologists, as one might reasonably expect, but from the now-declassified archives of the U.S. Army! Even weirder still, several eye witnesses to one of the encounters were from the U.S. Marine Corps—the very branch of the United States Armed Forces that Earl Morrison and his colleagues were with when they encountered the region's resident flying woman back in the summer of 1969.

Titled "'Sea Serpent' Sighting at Han River," the two-page document in question tells an extraordinary story. On the morning of September 17, 1965, several Marine Corps personnel, along with two personnel from the 311th Air Commando Squadron of the 315th Air Command Group, were flying by helicopter from Da Nang Air Base (today, the Da Nang International Airport) when, while crossing the Han River at low level, they caught sight of something incredible and almost primeval in the waters below. It was, they all later told an interviewing officer, a huge, serpentine creature, easily 80 feet in length. Bright yellow in color, it was swimming at a relatively slow rate of speed, and very near the surface, along the flowing waters of the river.

Could the creature have been nothing stranger than a large snake, the length of which the team had exaggerated, albeit innocently, in their state of excitement and amazement? No, not according to the eye witnesses: They claimed that the creature possessed four large flippers that, as a result of the striking color of the creature, could easily be seen against the background of the dark water. And they were flippers that, along with a powerful, flicking tail, appeared to be pushing the creature along as it swam.

The files also reveal that, given none of the men thought to take even a solitary, priceless photograph of the beast in the half minute or so that it was in view before quickly vanishing below the waves, some degree of discussion was given amongst superior officers to the possibility that the whole thing was nothing more than a good-natured hoax. Each and every one of the men was absolutely adamant that it most certainly was not a hoax, but they did concede that all thoughts of photographing the creature were eclipsed by the shocking sight of seeing such an immense animal in the first place. And, after all, how many of us can accurately predict the way in which we might react when confronted by such a beast of the deep? Perhaps, far more than a few of us might forget all about the camera in our pocket when faced with an 80-foot monster only mere feet below us.

Though the story was of some interest to the military, because it involved several of their very own—and highly-trained—personnel, it obviously had no bearing upon national security, and so the matter was simply and quickly forgotten about and became nothing more than a very curious and little-known aside in the history of the Vietnam War. But, there is one more thing that needs to be mentioned: The author of the document included a very brief footnote stating that institutional memory on-base revealed an extremely similar creature—even down to the pronounced yellow coloring—had been seen, also in the Han River, in the late summer of 1962, shortly after U.S. military personnel were assigned to the base to help monitor the activities of the Viet Cong.

There is something deeply strange about Vietnam's Han River. After all, how many places in the world have played host to a gigantic serpent of the deep, a flying, winged woman who glows a captivating shade of green, and a suicidal father returned as a glowing ball of light?

Deeply strange is a most apt description for the next place in our targets, too: a seemingly quaint and peaceful little town in the Lone Star State. But, it's not always quaint and peaceful. You've heard of the phrase "no rest for the wicked," right? Well, where we're about to go now, there's no rest for the dead. Or Bigfoot, for that matter!

13

Jefferson, Texas, USA

There can be very few—if, indeed, any—cities, towns, or villages in the world that do not have at least one ghostly legend attached to them. But, just occasionally, a locale can boast of not just one resident spirit, but a veritable army of the walking and wailing dead. One of those places is the old town of Jefferson, Texas. Located on the Lone Star State's Big Cypress Bayou, large wetlands on the western side of Caddo Lake, Jefferson has a history that is various parts rich and turbulent, but always weird.

At the height of the American Civil War of 1861 to 1865, the good folks of Jefferson, despite being adversely affected and dramatically scarred by the conflict, played a significant role in helping to ensure the Confederate Army did not go short of food, water, clothing, weapons, and whatever else was needed in the battle with Union forces. And although Jefferson and its people were galvanized into doing whatever they conceivably could for the war effort, it was a time of strife, turmoil, and tragedy for one and all.

In the immediate post-war years, however, the town of Jefferson, like so many others that had bore the brunt of war, began to slowly return to normality, and even thrive, when hundreds of people in the south, who had lost their homes as a result of the conflict, poured into town looking to start new lives. Six years after the war was over, the Bayou was booming: The townspeople were busy exporting bushels of seed, wool, and pelts by the ton, and cattle- and sheep-farming ensured Jefferson significant income. All was good…for a while, anyway.

Unfortunately, in very much the same way that Jefferson had suffered during the Civil war, it wouldn't be long before that suffering surfaced once again. Only a few years after Jefferson got back up on its feet, the U.S. Corps of Engineers elected to significantly lower the water-level of the Big Cypress Bayou, the effect of which was that the various boats and ships that used it as a means to transfer produce could no longer easily travel the waters that had suddenly become very shallow, and as a result, significantly treacherous. There was only one inevitable result: Unable to adequately and successfully export the very things that kept it alive, Jefferson began to suffer and decline. But, again, it pulled itself back from the brink and, today, can boast of being one of the most delightful, picturesque, and captivating of all of Texas's towns of eras long gone.

Packed with antique shops, inviting bed and breakfast establishments, spacious hotels that hark back to the days of old-time gunslingers, and horse-drawn carriages that take tourists around town on the original brick streets, Jefferson, today, really is a town out of time, or perhaps even one suspended in time. And, maybe, that goes for its many ghosts, too, the majority of which seem to have their origins in the times of old, and a significant number of which haunt a certain hotel.

The staff of the Jefferson Hotel talks of the couple that once stayed in Room Five, and whose young son was repeatedly awakened during the night by a phantom man wearing an old-time long coat and high leather boots. Strange, and somewhat disturbing, whispers and fragments of ghostly conversation can be heard in the hotel's corridors and rooms. A spooky, but vivacious blond woman haunts a particular bed in the hotel. So attached is she to that particular bed that when it was moved from Room 12 to Room 14, the woman—whose ethereal, golden hair is often reported seen shining in a cloud of mist—dutifully went with it. And guests report sudden, eerie drops in temperature in those rooms in which the dead are said to dwell. Not to be outdone in the spectral stakes, there is the equally varied body of spooks and ghostly phenomena that haunt the town's Excelsior Hotel on West Austin Street.

The haunted Jefferson Hotel, Texas (copyright Nick Redfern)

Built more than 150 years ago, the Excelsior is the second oldest hotel in town and has played host to such guests as Oscar Wilde, and Presidents Ulysses S. Grant and Lyndon B. Johnson. Even Steven Spielberg stayed there when he was directing his 1974 movie, *Sugarland Express*. Only a few nights in, however, he ordered all his crew to leave and find new rooms at a Holiday Inn, some 20 miles away. The reason, as Spielberg tactfully told it, was that he was sure his room was haunted. It was: by the spirit of a young boy who, legend says, asked Spielberg what he wanted for breakfast! Other guests are far stranger than a movie mogul, a couple of presidents, and an acclaimed writer, however.

Unlike the situation at the Jefferson Hotel, the staff at the Excelsior is not overly keen to promote its line-up of supernatural stars. But, they are there all the same. The Jay Gould room—named after a railroad entrepreneur of the 1800s, Jason "Jay" Gould—and its immediate corridor area has been the site of a headless, ghostly man. A disturbing specter in black, sometimes seen in the room cradling her phantom-baby, in a creaking rocking-chair no less, has scared the life out of more than a couple of guests, none of whom, it seems certain to say, were expecting *that* kind of greeting while staying at the Excelsior.

Demonstrating that matters of a mysterious nature are still afoot at the hotel, as recently as 2009, the spirit of what appeared to be a Confederate soldier was seen by a shocked couple from Dallas as its passed through their bedroom wall at the Excelsior. It's worth noting that this is not the only Civil War-themed spirit said to dwell in the heart of old Jefferson. The Claiborne House, on South Alley, was built in 1872 by V.H. Claiborne, a captain in the Confederate forces. And it seems he is highly reluctant to leave. A number of years ago, former owner, Karen Gleason, reported seeing an apparition in the house of a man dressed in a long coat, white shirt, and sporting an Abraham Lincoln-style beard. Several months later, her husband, Bill, saw the same thing. Later owners Steve and Elaine Holden did not see the captain, but they did experience ghostly activity: sudden drops in temperature and flickering lights.

Local historian Jodi Breckenridge invites people to attend her Friday and Saturday night *Historical Jefferson Ghost Walks* around town, where one and all can learn just about anything and everything there is to know about the specters of Jefferson. But, it's not just ghosts that comprise the weirdness that dominates Jefferson. Like all the places we have come to know so far, and those that are still to come, Jefferson is a hotbed of high strangeness.

Up until just a few years ago, Jefferson played host to the annual conference of the *Texas Bigfoot Research Conservancy*, which saw many of the leading experts in the field of monster-hunting giving yearly presentations on all-things relative to the famous hairy man-beast. And, based on what you are about to read, Bigfoot may very well have been mighty proud of the coverage it's gotten in Jefferson over the years, and decided to pay its people a visit.

Back in early September 1965, the local media highlighted the story of a hairy man-beast on the loose in and around Jefferson. It was on August 20th of that year that 13-year-old Johnny Maples was walking home from a friend's house, and it was a normal day; for a while, at least. Johnny was on FM 1784 between Prospect and Lodi, when he heard noises emanating from the adjacent bushes. He called out twice, thinking that perhaps it was someone pulling a prank. When there was no reply, however, Johnny became naturally concerned, picked up a couple of rocks, and hurled them into the brush. At that point a frightful, fiendish thing came storming out of the foliage and Johnny found himself face-to-face with a Bigfoot. According to the tale of the terrified boy, which was investigated by Marion County Deputy Sheriff, George Whatley, the creature was around 7 feet in height and covered in dark hair, aside from on its face, the palms of its hands, and its stomach. And although no evidence for the existence of the creature was ever found, it was clear to the investigating officers that the boy in question had been deeply traumatized by the presence of something. Maybe that something is still there.

Late one evening in March 2009, a truck-driver named Mark Duke was driving on the outskirts of Jefferson, heading for his final destination, which was just over the border in Louisiana, when he caught a brief glimpse of a large, hair-covered animal ambling across the road in an almost comical, casual fashion. Likening the creature to a big ape crossed with a lumbering bear, Duke said that at the time of its appearance, he was turning on a tight bend, and as a result, his speed was very slow—which, he said, gave him the ideal opportunity to see the beast very clearly. In his mind, there was no doubt: Jefferson is the haunt of Bigfoot.

And then there is the aforementioned Caddo Lake, upon the Big Cypress Bayou of which Jefferson is situated.

Caddo Lake is the largest natural freshwater lake in all of the south, covering approximately 26,800 acres. Originally home to the Caddo Indians (a friendly and peaceful tribe that hunted, fished, and made pottery), the lake's murky depths and incredibly dense black cypress trees help to create a truly spooky atmosphere within which Bigfoot is said to firmly thrive. And, make no mistake: encounters with North America's famous man-beast abound at Caddo Lake. Locally, it is known as the Caddo Critter. It's worth noting that such is its infamy, it has also made its presence felt in the world of on-screen fiction—specifically in a 1976 movie starring Jack Elam titled *The Creature from Black Lake,* about a violent, killer Bigfoot. One of those convinced that Bigfoot inhabited the lake was Charlie DeVore, who lived on Big Cypress Bayou since 1990. He spent a large amount of time searching for the beast, and on several occasions came across an overpowering stench in the area that he firmly believed to be the creature's scent.

Bigfoot, the ghosts of Confederate soldiers, a spirit without a head, and a hot, spooky blond: just some of the strange beings for which Jefferson, Texas, is a never-ending hang-out.

And there's another place where the dead are content to endlessly roam. Far from being a sleepy old Texan town, however, this one plays host to the ghosts of some of the most powerful and ruthless men to have ever lived.

14

Kremlin, Moscow, Russia

Deep in the heart of the Russian capital city of Moscow, and dominating the Moskva River, Red Square, and Saint Basil's Cathedral, stands the famous Moscow Kremlin. It's a majestic and historic structure that dates back to the 12th century, when the Grand Duke of Kiev, Yuri Dolgoruky, ordered the construction of a wooden fort in the area that laid the foundations of the city as it exists today. By the turn of the 14th century, the Kremlin, then under Ivan the Great, was massively expanded upon and fortified with stone walls. And Moscow, both in terms of its size and influence, both at home and abroad, began to steadily grow. Today, the Kremlin is comprised of four lavish palaces, an equal number of highly decorated cathedrals, and it operates as the official residence of the President of the Russian Federation. But, there's far more in residence at the Kremlin than a famous politician. The ghosts of Ivan the Terrible and premiers Vladimir Lenin and Josef Stalin are all said to roam the old corridors and rooms of the Kremlin, striking cold fear into all who are unfortunate enough to encounter them. And then there is the strange saga of Russia's very own equivalent of Roswell, which suggests the remains of an alien spacecraft are secretly held in a fortified room far below Russia's most famous and historic building.

As for the spirits of the Kremlin, let us begin with terrible Ivan himself, the Grand Prince of Moscow from 1533 to 1584. On several occasions, his ghostly form has reportedly been seen in what is called the Ivan the Great Bell Tower, a massive, 266-foot-high feature built in the 1500s in the Kremlin's Cathedral Square most notable for its huge, golden dome. But, the most fascinating story suggests that the spectral, grim-faced, and fire-enveloped form of Ivan the Terrible appeared briefly after the death of Alexander III, the Emperor of Russia from 1881 to 1894, and only one day before the coronation of the very last Russian Tsar, Nicolas II. The latter was a ghostly manifestation seen by some Kremlin staff as a shocking and worrying omen that the Romanov dynasty was destined not to last. And, as history has unfortunately shown, it most certainly didn't. It all ended in a quick, bloody, murderous mess in the early hours of July 17, 1918 when, at the Ipatiev House in the Russian city of Yekaterinburg, the tsar and his family were gruesomely shot and bayoneted by a firing-squad comprised of communist and Bolshevik soldiers under the command of a Bolshevik officer named Yakov Yurovsky.

When it comes to Vladimir Lenin, rather oddly, the first recorded appearance of his very own ghostly image in the Kremlin occurred while he was actually still alive! On the night in question, October 19, 1923, Lenin was laying deathly ill in his residence at Gorki. A guard, acutely aware of Lenin's precarious and fading state of health at the time, was shocked and amazed to see what appeared to be a strong, vibrant, and even young-looking Lenin striding through the corridors of the Kremlin when it was assumed he was struggling to hang on to his life. A highly puzzled duty officer placed a hasty call to Gorki, where staff quickly confirmed the premier was indeed seriously ill and strictly confined to his room, and most definitely not roaming around the presidential residence. So, who or what *was* wandering around the Kremlin? An impostor, an enemy of the state, or maybe something even stranger and possibly even supernatural? Rumors rapidly spread that perhaps Lenin, wishing to see his beloved Kremlin one more time, and knowing that his time on this plain of existence was running perilously short (he died barely three months later), underwent some form of out-of-body experience, in which his soul or essence traveled to the Kremlin and was briefly encountered by a shocked guard on late-night duty.

Perhaps it was such was such a strong tie that Lenin had to the Kremlin that, after his passing, some paranormal aspect of his existence remained, destined to never leave the old, historic building. In 2004, Sergei Kuleshov, a noted historian, was working at the Kremlin-based President's Archives and had the opportunity to speak with a KGB colonel who was a wealth of data on stories of unexplained noises, footsteps, and what sounded like heavy furniture being moved in Lenin's locked study. A near-identical claim was made by Sergei Filatov, the Chief of President's Staff under Boris Yeltsin, who experienced such unsettling sounds on a number of occasions in 1993. No explanation was ever forthcoming. Or, at least, no *normal* explanation was ever forthcoming.

Then there is Josef Stalin, who ruthlessly held sway over the former Soviet Union from 1941 to 1953. For such an ice-cold ruler, it's highly appropriate that those who claim to have seen the ghost of Stalin walking the old rooms and hallways of the Kremlin say that when he manifests, a dramatic drop in temperature occurs at the very same time. Most terrifying of all, when Stalin appears, any open doors and windows in the immediate vicinity are suddenly slammed and locked, as if by some macabre force that wishes to ensure those for whom the old premier manifests cannot escape his cold and malevolent stare and wrath.

Now, we leave the dead of the Kremlin behind and move on to the aliens of the old building.

In yet another intriguing twist in the seemingly never-ending saga of the Roswell UFO crash in 2011, a new and undeniably bizarre theory for what happened in the summer of 1947 on the Foster Ranch, in Lincoln County, New Mexico, surfaced. Although the UFO research community, for the most part, believes that aliens from a world far away met their deaths on that long-gone day, and the U.S. Air Force stubbornly maintains that nothing stranger than balloon-based debris and crash-test dummies were found, the latest story provided a very different answer to the riddle of Roswell. It came from a woman named

Annie Jacobsen, an American journalist, who had been told—by Alfred O'Donnell, a 90-year-old U.S. defense contractor and former employee of Edgerton, Germeshausen, and Grier, Inc (EG&G)—that the Roswell bodies were neither extraterrestrial nor dummies. In reality, she was carefully and quietly advised, they were the diabolical creations of a secret pact between Dr. Josef Mengele—a notorious wartime Nazi scientist known as the Angel of Death—and Soviet premier Joseph Stalin, who planned and weaved a brilliant ruse from right in the heart of his office in the Kremlin.

Aliens, ghosts, and a crashed UFO: all parts of the mystery of the Kremlin. (copyright, Shardusky, 1840s)

The purpose of this early, secret Cold War affair, Jacobsen's source earnestly informed her, was to plunge the United States into a *War of the Worlds*-style panic by trying to convince the U.S. government that aliens were invading. And how was the plan expected to work? By placing grossly deformed children—courtesy of the crazed Mengele—inside a futuristic-looking aircraft, and then remotely flying it to the United

States. The purpose: to convince the United States of the alien origins of both. So O'Donnell told it, unfortunately for Stalin, the plot failed when a violent storm brought down the craft and its crew in the wilds of the New Mexico desert, an event that did not lead to widespread panic after all, but was hastily covered up by senior U.S. military authorities in the Pentagon and at the former Roswell Army Air Field.

It must be noted that the story is a highly controversial one that even the most vociferous of all skeptics of the notion that aliens crashed at Roswell have a hard time accepting as valid. But, the story does serve to demonstrate a potential tie in between the UFO phenomenon and the Kremlin. And this is not the only 1947-themed affair that leads us to the very heart of that famous Moscow-based complex.

According to data uncovered and revealed by Russian UFO researcher Anton Anfalov, in the summer of 1947, and during the rebuilding of the city of Kiev, which had been decimated by the Nazis during World War II, workers discovered a mysterious 16- to 20-foot-long metal object buried underground and described as being silver in color, lacking any seams or rivets, and shaped like an arrow. Reportedly, the object was carefully and secretly excavated and a team of military personnel was quickly brought in to transfer it to a classified location somewhere northeast of Moscow—where it was subsequently studied by some of the finest minds in the field of Soviet aerospace research and technology.

Astonishingly, the object was not—as had been initially assumed by many—a secret spy-plane of the United States that had gone awry high in the skies over Russia, slamming into the ground, but something stranger. First, scientists concluded that it had remained buried for 5,000 years, which effectively rules out the hand of modern man having played a role in its construction. And second, when the scientific team finally managed to find a way to access the interior of the object, they found a pair of chairs designed for very small personnel, as well as a wide variety of highly advanced technologies that were studied by Russia's scientific elite. According to Anfalov, careful studies were undertaken from the 1950s to the 1970s, which helped to advance Soviet missile and space technology, including the development of advanced alloys, instrumentation, and construction techniques.

There is an intriguing footnote to this story: V.L. Durov, formerly of the Soviet KGB, says that, in 1987, the craft in question was ultimately transferred—via a series of very deep underground rail systems designed to ferry and protect senior government and military personnel in the event of a nuclear strike on Moscow—to a large and secure bunker buried far below the Kremlin. If Durov is correct, then Area 51, it seems, is not the only place on our planet alleged to secretly harbor spacecraft from other galaxies. And the UFO links to the Kremlin most certainly do not end there. Indeed, they extend right up to the present day.

On December 9, 2009, an amazing story broke of a vast, near-mile-wide, pyramid- or triangular-shaped UFO seen directly over the Kremlin by two independent sources. Such was the amazement, furore, and publicity given to the case—which was supported by hundreds of additional eyewitnesses—it even led Nick Pope, formerly an investigator of UFO sightings and reports for the British Ministry of Defense, to go on the record with a few choice and memorable words. Commenting on one of the pieces of film-footage obtained that day was carefully scrutinized, Pope said that, in his opinion, it represented one of the most extraordinary pieces of UFO-themed footage he had ever had the opportunity to view. And although skeptics suggested that both films showed nothing stranger than mere lens reflection of a down-to-earth object, the story refused to roll over and die. It was revealed that on the very same night, a blue-colored aerial spiral of light was seen high in the skies of parts of northern Norway and Sweden.

Although UFOs and meteors were quickly suggested as the culprits in this case, the Russian Navy maintained that the mysterious aerial manifestation was caused by a failed test of one of its submarine-based RSM-56 Bulava missiles. Flying saucer enthusiasts were hardly, if even at all, impressed by such a claim, however. And, noting the tie-in with the encounter over the Kremlin on the same precise evening, they championed the notion that alien visitors from afar were putting on a distinct show of power by turning up above the official residence of the President of the Russian Federation. And, if that was the case, then maybe they chose to return and demonstrate their might once more. In 2011, *another*

UFO appeared above the Kremlin and once again attracted sensational and widespread coverage and commentary.

On the weekend of December 10–11, 2011, a major protest was held in Moscow, at which more than 25,000 people voiced their anger at the government of Vladimir Putin. But, attentions were soon diverted from the president to the skies. High above the Kremlin was a strange, hovering craft that many claimed provided clear and undeniable evidence that we are not alone in the universe. But this was no regular flying saucer. Rather, it was cylinder-shaped and appeared to possess legs and what looked suspiciously like rotor-blades—not unlike those one would ordinarily see on a helicopter. In view of its description, might the UFO actually have been some form of highly sophisticated spy-drone of the Russian Government, and of a type similar to those used more and more by the U.S. military on and above the battlefields of the Middle East?

Some suggested that this is *exactly* what was seen, and that its presence was to carefully and specifically film the protestors and identify potential troublemakers in the crowd. If this was indeed so, then this affair clearly serves to demonstrate that when it comes to UFOs, differentiating between what might be one of *our* UFOs and one of *theirs* (whoever *they* may well be) is going to become an increasingly difficult task as our military technology advances. But, of one thing we can be certain: regardless of the true origin of the mysterious vehicle of December 2011, it only adds to the mystique and controversy concerning the link between overwhelming weirdness and the Kremlin.

Let's now leave behind us the mysteries of Moscow and get hot on the trail of monsters. There's something in the woods...

15

Laguna, Philippines, Southeast Asia

The Republic of the Philippines, which is a collection of 7,107 islands in the western Pacific Ocean, sits between Taiwan and Vietnam. Its people claim it is absolutely overflowing with just about anything and everything of a weird and enigmatic nature. And that is particularly so in the province of Laguna, which is situated in the Calabrazon region of Luzon, the largest island in the Philippines. After all, how many places on our planet can claim amongst its varied supernatural residents the following: real-life dragons, gigantic birds with huge wingspans; goblins and dwarfs (or, as they are known in the Philippines, the Nuno sa Punso and the Duende); one-eyed giants (Cyclops-type beasts); and a multitude of vampires whose appearances include those of a beautiful woman, a hideous, fetus-like being, and the bat-winged Manananggal?

Laguna is the perfect setting for an absolute menagerie of bizarre entities to inhabit. A deep waterfall, the Pagsanjan Falls, dominates the area. Two long-dormant volcanoes, Mount Banahaw and Mount Makiling, lie to the south. And the province itself sits on the southernmost shores of Laguna de Bay, the biggest lake in the entire Philippines. It's amid this picturesque and captivating environment that terrible things roam, swim, and soar. Let's start with those creatures that science and zoology tells us simply cannot exist, but that the folk of the area most assuredly suggest otherwise: fire-breathing dragons.

The Mameleu is a huge snake—one whose length is reputed to reach almost 200 feet when fully grown. Atop its head sits a large and powerful horn capable of inflicting very serious damage on anyone who dares to get in its way. It's also a creature that shoots flames out of its cavernous jaws and whose evil-looking eyes glow a constant fiery red. A sea-dwelling beast, the Mameleu has reportedly been seen to prowl the waters of Laguna de Bay by the light of a full moon, carefully and hungrily scanning the rolling waters for a tasty fisherman or several. And, the people of Laguna say it has a land-based cousin: the Marcupo, a very similar-looking monster with a devilish forked-tail. Then there is the mighty Baconaua, a silver-colored dragon of immense size that soars across the skies of Laguna thanks to the power of its gigantic, bat-like, membranous wings. To demonstrate the sheer size of Baconaua, local mythology says that in the very distant past our planet had seven moons, of which Baconaua greedily devoured six, leaving us with just one to call our own.

And, now, from monsters massive, to creatures distinctly small.

The Nuno sa Punso are secretive and shy dwarfish creatures that, in the folklore of Laguna, live deep inside discarded, old ant hills. Having the appearance of wizened, old men with red-hued skin and long, flowing beards, they very much keep to themselves—that is, unless someone makes the monumental mistake of disturbing their hilly homes. Then all hell breaks loose. The goblin-like Nuno sa Punso are very practiced at placing one particular curse upon people who dare to cross them, and it's a curse that surely no-one would wish to endure, particularly because it causes swelling of the face and hands, excessive hair growth all over the body, and will even turn your urine black! In other words, if you happen to visit Laguna, stay the hell away from the ant hills.

Somewhat Nuno sa Punso-like are the Duende: little figures that also bear an uncanny resemblance to wrinkled old men, but who possess only one eye and live under trees rather than in the nests of ants. They are cold-hearted creatures that trade gold for children, and stealthily break into homes late at night and steal newborn babies. Should you ever encounter a Duende, the people of Laguna say, shower the beast in salt. And, finally, on the matter of the miniscule entities of the Philippines, we come to the Kibaan. They are a decidedly odd bunch, with golden-colored teeth, feet that face backward, and heads of thick hair that reach to the ground. They are said to construct and play their very own, tiny, guitar-like instruments while sitting in the trees amongst their favorite of all friends: fireflies. Now to monsters of the skies.

In Laguna lurks a legendary one-eyed monster: a Cyclops (Copyright Odilon Redon, 1914)

Sounding very much like the type of unlikely creatures that Godzilla would do valiant battle with in an old Japanese monster-movie, the Mikonawa and Bawa are massive, winged things with beaks and talons made of pure steel, and feathers as strong, long, and deadly as the average sword that King Arthur would have been proud to own. Just like the Baconaua, they, too, both have a curious penchant for devouring entire moons. There is one way to prevent these monstrous, bird-like beasts from having a catastrophic chow down on the solar system, however: Place a welcoming bowl of hot and tasty food outside of your front door late at night, or gently lull them into a pleasant slumber with an inviting local, folk tune.

Tales of bands of one-eyed giants (Cyclops-like creatures) abound, also. The Bungusngis are known for being as large as they are stupid. With a single eye protruding from their foreheads and huge tusks dominating their mouths, they roam the wilds of the land in search of water buffalo—their favorite morsel.

The Amomongo is a goliath-sized, gorilla-like animal of a most violent nature that will slaughter and devour pretty much anyone or anything that has the misfortune to get in its path. Interestingly, witness reports from the vicinity of the old volcanoes suggest the creature has far more than a passing resemblance to Bigfoot of the United States. And possibly of relevance to the Amomongo are the Kapre, also a species of hair-covered giants. Rather than being hostile to humans, however, they are genial and gentle folk who are most at home when devouring raw tobacco or smoking huge cigars!

Then there are those creatures of Laguna that seem to almost completely defy any sort of classification whatsoever. A perfect example is the Tikbalangs. They are tall, humanoid entities that have the head and hooves of a horse, and legs so long that, when they sit, their knees rise above their heads. Though not specifically malicious or aggressive, they are definitive tricksters. Tikbalangs take particular pleasure in leading people astray, getting them lost in the woods, and generally causing disorientation and distress whenever and wherever possible. Most bizarre of all, however, are the Sigbin. Resembling white-haired, hornless goats, they have huge ears that they clap together as a means to warn others of their kind of impending danger. They also walk backward, and slaughter by licking the shadow of their prey.

Now, from the bizarre, let's turn to the downright deadly: Laguna's vampires.

The Tiyanak is a terrifying creature of the night that resembles a human fetus and cries like a human baby to attract and lure its prey to a horrific death—very much like the giant Svokan of the Caucasus Mountains. Also of a nocturnal and bloodsucking nature are the Balbal. They fly and glide through the moonlit skies of Laguna with only one goal in mind: to seek out the homes of the recently departed. Then, when they find such a place, and their powerful nostrils alert them to the fact that the body is still in evidence, they wildly tear off the roofs of the buildings, and hang from the rafters by their vicious-looking talons, eagerly on the lookout for both body and blood. And on finding both, the Tiyanak extend their coiling, long tongues downward and proceed to excitedly lick the corpses of the unfortunate people, a process via which massive amounts of blood can be extracted to fuel their soulless forms. Even worse than the Tiyanak is the Manananggal: by day, the loathsome thing appears in the form of a beautiful, alluring woman. By night, however, it transforms into a hideous hag replete with matted hair, a hooked nose, long claws, and yellowy fangs. On achieving its vile transformation, the Manananggal takes to the skies in search of fresh flesh on which to feed—but not before detaching the lower part of its body from the upper section, a process which ensures that those who are unfortunate enough to see the creature soaring overhead are witness to the unforgettable and awful sight of its bloody entrails hanging and swaying wildly below. And, finally, there is the Asuang: a shape-shifting sucker of blood that can take on the form of a pig, bird, cat, or dog. It is not at all averse to mercilessly slicing open the stomachs of pregnant women and devouring their unborn children.

And there we have it: Laguna, a land filled to the brim with bizarre and deadly monsters, none of which it would be at all wise to cross paths with.

So much for land that brims with weirdness: we're about to get our feet wet again as we return to the water. In fact, we're going to the very heart and depths of one of the most infamous of all lakes in the world. It's a place that is home to one very well-known enigma and to a host of other, lesser-known ones. But, all of them are, of course, weird.

16

Loch Ness, Scotland

Approximately 250 million years ago, massive and violent changes in the Earth's crust carved a gigantic rift across a specific area of the landscape of Scotland, which has since become known as the Great Glen. During many millennia, the huge, basin-like Glen began to fill with water, and eventually transformed much of the country into an area populated by more than 31,000 lakes—or lochs, as they are known to the Scots. And, without doubt, the most famous of all those is Loch Ness, the dark and mysterious abode of the legendary long-necked monster dubbed Nessie. In excess of 20 miles long, nearly a mile wide, around 755 feet deep, and home to the famous Urquhart Castle (the origins of which date back to the 6th century), Loch Ness is a distinctly eerie and magical place. And, unknown to most people, it is a loch populated to bursting point with numerous stories of a supernatural nature that have little, if anything, to do with the monstrous enigma said to lurk in its deep, dark waters.

But before we get to those other mysterious legends of the loch, let's start, as we surely must, with Nessie. For decades (some would argue for centuries) sightings have been made by literally thousands of people of what appear to be large, aquatic animals living and thriving in Loch Ness. Typically, witnesses describe seeing a beast—or, very occasionally, several beasts together—with a muscular, humped back, an elongated neck that stands proudly out of the water, powerful flippers, and sometimes a thrashing tail. Incredibly, a handful of reports exist of people even claiming to have seen the beast basking on the ancient shores of Loch Ness, seemingly sunning its elephant-like skin. So, unless all of those people are simply hoaxers, the victims of pranks, or have innocently misinterpreted sightings of known animals such as seals, sturgeon, and catfish (which have all been put forward as candidates to try and explain the controversy), the biggest and most important question is: What are they seeing? The theories are many. The hard evidence, unfortunately, is far less so.

There can be no doubt that the most popular theory is that the creatures of Loch Ness represent a colony of plesiosaurs: aquatic reptiles that science assures us met their collective end during the Cretaceous period, some 65.5 million years ago. Certainly, the long neck, the raised back, and the flippers that were all typical of the plesiosaur suggest this creature, perhaps more than any other, would be a viable candidate for Nessie. And, the country's tourist-board, is, of course, always pleased to promote the idea that *Jurassic Park*-like monsters dwell deep in the loch. There are, however, big problems: Plesiosaurs are believed to have been coldblooded animals requiring distinctly tropical climates in which to live. They also lived in the oceans, which are filled with salt water. Averaging 41 degrees Farenheit, Loch Ness is anything but tropical, and is fresh water. And the resident fish population of Loch Ness is hardly sufficient to nourish, on a daily basis, a large colony of flesh-eating creatures, some of which, the fossil record demonstrates, grew to lengths in excess of 65 feet.

Then there is the theory that the beasts might be gigantic eels. An engaging idea, and not impossible, but eels do not typically have the ability to raise their heads and necks out of the water in the fashion famously attributed to Nessie. Nor do they grow to lengths of 30 or 40 feet.

Others have suggested whales as candidates. As whales are mammals, however, they would need to surface for air on regular occasions, thus ensuring they would be seen far more often. So, we have a big conundrum. And it's a conundrum that has led more than a few people to conclude that the creatures of Loch Ness may not be flesh and blood beasts at all, but might have paranormal origins.

The plesiosaur: a candidate for the Loch Ness Monster (copyright Heinrich Harder, 1916)

While digging deep into the subject of the U.S. government's secret research into the realms of so-called remote viewing and psychic spying, the well-known authority on conspiracy theories, Jim Marrs, learned that elements of the official world had secretly attempted to focus their skills upon solving the riddle of what it is that lurks within the deep and dark waters of Loch Ness. It was a very controversial operation, however, as Marrs noted. And it led to an amazing conclusion:

> Several sessions targeting the famous Loch Ness monster revealed physical traces of the beast—a wake in the water, movement of a large body underwater. Their drawings even resembled a prehistoric plesiosaur, often identified as matching descriptions of Nessie. But when the viewers tried to discover where the object came from

or returned to, they hit a dead end. The creature seemed
to simply appear and disappear." (Marrs)

Incredibly, Marrs revealed, it was this curious issue that led the remote-viewers to form the opinion that Nessie might actually represent the ghost of a long-dead dinosaur. Most people might scoff at such a theory, but if true, it would certainly not be out of place with respect to the large body of additional paranormal activity at the loch. In fact, it would be right at home, as now becomes clear.

Moving away from Nessie, there's another great beast of Loch Ness to deal with: Aleister Crowley. It may amaze many to know that Crowley, one of the world's most infamous occultists, and a devotee of all-things supernatural, alchemical, and magical, once owned a property at Loch Ness. An old hunting lodge constructed back in the 1700s, its name is Boleskine House and it became Crowley's place of residence from 1899 to 1913. It was while living at Boleskine House, which still stands to this day, on the southeast shore of Nessie's haunt, that Crowley embarked upon a magical ritual to provoke conversation with what he termed the holy guardian angel. The process was a torturous and intense one for Crowley. And so claimed the Great Beast, it worked; but not in a positive fashion.

Crowley told of how the hostile and malevolent actions of ominous spirits that he personally summoned at Loch Ness resulted in a maid fleeing the house, never to return, and a local tradesman plunging into the depths of irreversible insanity. And in somewhat proud terms, Crowley offered that a successful attempt on his part to invoke literal demons at the loch led to the death of a local butcher. The man, said Crowley, accidentally, but fatally, severed a major artery while working and bled to death on the cold, stone floor of his store. So the story went, Crowley had written the names of certain deadly demons on a receipt from the butcher's store, thus condemning the man to a tragic and, quite literally, bloody end.

Just across from the residence is an old cemetery, one said to be haunted by malevolent spirits. And, longstanding rumor suggests that an old tunnel links Boleskine House to the graveyard; a tunnel which used to act as a secret safe haven for a witch coven that operated in the area during the 1700s and 1800s. The other most famous resident of the creepy old house was Jimmy Page, guitarist for the band *Led Zeppelin*, who also commented on the negative atmosphere and disturbing vibes that permeated the house and its immediate surroundings.

On May 2, 2000, the folk who live around Loch Ness were alerted to a spate of savage mutilations and killings of sheep by what at least three witnesses described as a fully grown puma. Such was the overwhelming concern shown as a result of the incidents that Northern Constabulary wildlife liaison officer John Cathcart warned local farmers to take extra care of their sheep, particularly newborn lambs. Something large, predatory, and hungry was prowling around Loch Ness by night—and it most certainly was not Nessie. For a couple of weeks, things were mercifully quiet. But by the end of May, the mystery attacker was back again, and in deadly force. Farmer Davie MacLean found, to his absolute horror, a dead ewe and two lambs on his farm. All that was left of the poor animals were the skins, three torn-off heads, and a few bones that gave every indication of being viciously snapped by something possessed of powerful, muscular jaws. And the monstrous mayhem showed no signs of stopping. Further killings were reported in the direct vicinity of the loch, and, as June and July arrived, yet more sheep remains were discovered—this time near the shore of the loch itself, which did make a few locals wonder if the monster of the waters was to blame, rather than a big cat of the surrounding woods.

But, as intriguing as that latter scenario most certainly was, it was thrown into doubt when, in September 2001, a puma-like animal—possibly the very same one that had been responsible for all the mayhem in the summer of 2000—was seen by a civil engineer named David Straube, who nearly collided with the beast on a stretch of road near Kinnoir Woods. The creature did not hang around, however. It shot across the lane and bounded away into the trees. Fortunately, as this encounter had occurred during the morning, rather than on a dark and shadowy night, Straube was able to get a very good view of the beast and was certain it was not merely an overweight house cat. Nessie, it seems safe to say, is not the only unknown animal that haunts the ancient loch.

With stories of giant eels, still-surviving plesiosaurs, ghostly dinosaurs, and big cats all in evidence at Loch Ness, could things get any weirder? Yes, and particularly so when we bring real life fairies into the mix. On a blisteringly hot summer's morning in June 1981, Harry Mann was driving past the loch toward Inverness, when in front of his vehicle, at a distance of maybe 80 or 90 feet, materialized a small entity, dressed in bright green attire. Fortunately, Mann was driving at a slow pace, but instinctively slammed on the brakes, came to a rapid halt, and stared open-mouthed at the sight before him. According to Mann, the being was very human-like, had a wide grin on his face, and two large, near-transparent, insect-like wings that protruded from his back and above his head, which, in turn, was covered by a small green cap. For all intents and purposes, Mann was staring at a creature that, we are told, is a fairy.

The encounter, however, did not last for long—barely seconds. As Mann looked on even more astonished, quite understandably unsure of what his next move should be, the little fellow in green bowed gracefully, waved, and soared off into the skies, in the direction of the loch. Realizing how ridiculous he would appear should he ever dare tell anyone of his early morning encounter with one of the legendary little people, Harry Mann stayed absolutely silent on the matter until 2007. And, it was another Loch Ness-related event involving fairies, in a roundabout way, that prompted Mann to finally reveal all.

On May 26, 2007, a man named Gordon Holmes, a British lab technician, secured intriguing film footage of a large, black-colored creature, somewhere in the region of 45 feet in length, moving at a fast pace in the waters of Loch Ness. When the footage hit the Internet, it became clear that Holmes was not joking or exaggerating with respect to his description. But, as thought-provoking as the footage most certainly was, it was quickly overshadowed by Holmes' claim to have previously encountered a big cat—not unlike the one that terrorized the Loch Ness area in 2000 and 2001—and to have a firm belief in the existence of fairies. Although the media made a great deal of light of such revelations, for Harry Mann, Gordon Holmes was a kindred spirit and one who, although the two never met, prompted Mann to finally go public with his amazing tale of the little man of the loch.

Back in September 1978, Pete Smithson had a very odd, supernatural experience at Loch Ness. On the day at issue, Smithson was at the shore of the loch just when dawn was breaking, and was keen to capture a few photographs of the picturesque waters. Such thoughts went quickly out of the window, however, when Smithson was faced with the extraordinary sight of a man coming toward him. Not along the shore, as one might expect, but out the very depths of the loch itself. And, given that the man was dressed in a military uniform of the type worn by pilots, Smithson's first thought was that there had been some sort of accident, a plane had come down in the loch, and the man in question was a lucky, but very shocked survivor. Well, it was not quite that simple.

As the man got closer, Smithson could see that his uniform, rather than looking like one of a modern-day pilot, was far more befitting the type used by the British Royal Air Force during World War II, which, by then, had already been over for more than 30 years. That the man was dragging a parachute behind him in the water, only added to the unsettling atmosphere. As the curious figure began to exit the water and got closer to Smithson, he—the enigmatic airman—suddenly staggered, in a fashion that suggested he was about to faint, at which point Smithson felt a sudden chill overwhelm his body. He continued to watch, not at all sure how to handle the odd situation, but inquired of the man if he was okay or needed help. There was no reply. In fact, the man's only response to Smithson's questions was to point, in total silence, toward the deep loch, and then to suddenly vanish into thin air.

A ghostly airman killed during the hostilities of World War II, one whose soul was destined to forever haunt Loch Ness? Very possibly. On New Year's Eve, 1940, the crew of a British Royal Air Force Vickers Wellington aircraft found itself caught in a snowstorm over the loch that caused its engine to catastrophically fail. There was no choice, and all aboard raced to bail out. All survived except one, the tail-gunner, whose parachute failed to open properly. Was Pete Smithson's early morning visitor that very same doomed tail-gunner? We will probably never know, but such a sensational possibility should not be dismissed. After all, as we have seen, the weird secrets of Loch Ness run just about as long and deep as the loch itself.

Given that we are, after all, taking about Loch Ness, the home to the world's most famous of all lake monsters, it's only appropriate that we end where we started: with the monster. Or, maybe that should be *monsters*. Certainly, one of the most confounding, but certainly lesser-known things about the Loch Ness Monster is that a number of witnesses claim to have seen creatures in the loch that, though clearly of an unusual nature and extraordinary appearance, look nothing like the long-necked, humpbacked beasts that are most associated with the legendary Nessie. Could it be that incredibly, and against all the very odds, Loch Ness is home to *several* types of unknown animals, rather than just one? Such a scenario most certainly stretches credulity to its absolute limit, but that doesn't necessarily make it wrong.

Back in 1932, Miss K. MacDonald encountered a truly bizarre creature in the River Ness—which flows out of Loch Ness and toward the town of Inverness—that, she said, looked very much like a crocodile in shape and size, but sported a very short neck and even a pair of tusks! Clearly, there should not be any such mystifying animal swimming in the waters of either Loch Ness or the adjoining River Ness. Or, I scarcely need to say, anywhere in Scotland, period.

Six years later, a young girl named Alice Davenhill and her family encountered something equally monstrous and abominable, this time near Urquhart Castle, which happens to overlook a particular portion of the loch at which numerous sightings of the monster have been made. The family was strolling down to the shore for a picnic and evidently disturbed something that was basking at the water's edge. As with the case of Miss MacDonald back in 1932, the beast that the Davenhills encountered looked nothing like the typical image most people have of Nessie. Rather, it was only about 12 feet in length, had four short, fat legs—instead of the often-reported flippers—and two huge eyes that stared forth from a bulbous, wide head. Interestingly, Alice Davenhill recalled that, as the creature made its escape and headed toward the water, it seemed to have a very hard time doing so, as if land was hardly its natural environment. She elaborated that this was evidenced by its curious, almost comical, waddling-like gait as it sought to escape into the depths of Loch Ness, which it ultimately did, never to be seen again. The idea of hanging out for a pleasant picnic, unsurprisingly, was quickly abandoned.

And there we have it: A world-famous loch, housing an equally world-famous monster. But, on closer inspection, we can see that things aren't quite as simple as they first appear to be. Nessie, it becomes clearer and clearer the more we penetrate the heart of the paranormal puzzle, is actually just one of many enigmas in evidence in and around those dark, foreboding waters. That those same additional enigmas include fairies; big cats; horned and waddling beasts of an unearthly nature; phantom military personnel; a genial fairy; one of the world's most famous oc-cultists; demons; a haunted cemetery; and a coven of witches, tells us that, in the weird stakes, Loch Ness most certainly takes some beating.

There is a place that comes a close second to Loch Ness, however. Some might even say it eclipses the antics of Nessie and Co. in the seri-ously weird stakes. Come with me; we're going mountain climbing...

17

Mount Shasta, California, USA

Situated on the southern tip of the vast and mountainous Cascade Range, which encompasses parts of British Columbia, California, Washington State, and Oregon, Mount Shasta is a huge, all-dominating peak that, at nearly 15,000 feet, is the fifth tallest mountain in the Golden State, and one that has been home to human civilization, in varying degrees, since around 5,000 BC. It's also a mountain steeped in matters mysterious, unearthly, and deeply ancient.

On this latter point, Native American lore of the Klamath tribe tells of how, thousands of years ago, a mighty and turbulent battle was fought between Llao, the deity of the Underworld, and Skell, the Klamath's god of the skies. According to folklore, Llao found a way to exit the terrible world below via a portal in Mount Mazama (also on the Cascade Range) and succeeded in traveling to the stars, where Skell dwelled, provoking outright, hostile confrontation in the process. As a result, when Llao returned to Mazama, so Skell, too, descended from the heavens, to Mount Shasta, and a frightful war began. Such was the destructive and thunderous nature of the violent conflict between the gods that Mount Mazama erupted, leading to the creation of what is famously known today as Crater Lake. And, as punishment for daring to take on Skell in cosmic combat, and having been defeated, Llao was banished back to the darkest depths of the Underworld.

Moving on, but still on matters of a Native American nature, Hopi legend tells of a race of lizard-like people that built 13 underground cities along the Pacific Coast thousands of years ago, one of which, it is claimed, exists deep within the cavernous bowels of Mount Shasta. Then there are the Miwok and Siskiyou Indians, both of whose folklore maintains that a race of invisible people, rather than lizard folk, roam the area—both above and underground.

More than a century ago, Italian settlers, who had moved to the United States and worked in the fields of stonemasonry, laid the corner-stones of a soon-thriving Catholic community on Mount Shasta. And, in 1970, a Buddhist monastery, Shasta Abbey, was created by Houn Jiyu (who held the title of Roshi, a Japanese term meaning Elder Master or Old Teacher) and continues to offer visitors and disciples an abundance of data and teachings on all matters of a Buddhist nature.

As well as being a haven for a whole variety of religious teachings and beliefs, Mount Shasta is, as shall soon become clear, also the realm of Bigfoot and, as widespread belief suggests, the last vestiges of a mighty, renowned race of legendary people that once dominated the planet. They were known as the Lemurians and were said to have inhabited a now-sunken land, possibly situated somewhere in either the Pacific or Indian Ocean. Although the people of Lemuria reportedly attained their peak millennia ago, it was not until the late 19th century, and through the middle years of the 20th century, that they caught the public's attention on a large scale—and particularly so in relation to a certain connection with Mount Shasta. Truly, the story is a swirling cauldron of deep strangeness.

Back in the 1800s, Helen Blavatsky, the co-founder with William Quan Judge and Colonel Henry S. Olcott of the Theosophical Society (the original mandate of which was the study and elucidation of occultism), claimed to have been exposed to an ancient text of mysterious proportions that was said to have pre-dated the times and people of Atlantis.

Its title was the *Book of Dzyan* and was guarded with paranoid zeal by a brotherhood of powerful and ancient proportions. As a result of her reported exposure to the old and mighty tome, and while in Tibet studying esoteric lore, Blavatsky developed a remarkable framework concerning, and a belief in, the Lemurians that ultimately led to the very heart of Mount Shasta itself.

According to Blavatsky's findings, the Lemurians were the type of people for whom the phrase *once seen, never forgotten* might justifiably have been created. Around 7 feet in height, they were egg-laying hermaphrodites that, while not overly mentally developed, were, spiritually speaking, far more advanced than those who came before them. As Blavatsky described it, the Lemurians were the Third Root Race of a total of seven who were ultimately destroyed by appalled and angered gods after they, the people of Lemuria, turned to bestiality, and in doing so sealed their doom, around 12,500 BC. But, the gods were not done with life on Earth: They soon embarked on the creation of a Fourth Root Race, the equally legendary Atlanteans. Little did the gods realize it when they set about the creation of a new race, some of the Lemurians escaped the destruction and made their secret way to—as you may by now have guessed—a certain mountain in the Cascades.

The revelations of Blavatsky were elaborated on to a considerable degree by a British theosophist named William Scott-Elliot. He, in turn, had acquired his data from yet another theosophist, Charles Webster Leadbeater, who claimed clairvoyant communication with spiritually advanced, supernatural masters that imparted a wealth of data on both Lemuria and Atlantis. Also hot on the heels of Blavatsky, and only six years before the dawning of the 20th Century, a teenager named Frederick Spencer Oliver completed the writing of his book *A Dweller on Two Planets*. Published in 1905, six years after Oliver's untimely and very early death, the book caused a firestorm of controversy with its claims that the Lemurians shared a lineage with the Atlanteans, and that those Lemurians that escaped the pummeling wrath of the gods made their secret and collective way to Mount Shasta; just as Blavatsky had asserted. And they weren't just living *on* the mountain, but deep *within* it, too, in secret, cavernous depths that Oliver claimed could be accessed if one only knew the specific and secret entrance points of old. If one should ever encounter a tall, white-robed figure on Mount Shasta, said Oliver, it was all but certain to be a Lemurian.

And how, exactly, did Oliver know all this? Well, he claimed to have been in contact with a being that called itself Phylos the Tibetan. Phylos, whose controversial data was imparted to Oliver by a mind-to-mind process known as channeling, was said to have lived a number of lives or incarnations; one as a Lemurian and another as an Atlantean. Phylos also claimed to have reincarnated as Walter Pierson, a gold prospector who maintained he had seen a huge temple inside Mount Shasta. It was a structure that seemed to be practically constructed out of gold, silver, copper, precious ores, and priceless stones, and one that, today, would surely provoke definitive *Raiders of the Lost Ark*-style imagery and adventures.

As controversial as the story of Pierson most certainly sounded, it was one that received support from yet another prospector, J.C. Brown, who reported seeing a very similar structure deep inside the mountain in 1904. But Brown had another revelation, too. Strewn across the floor of the temple were the aged skeletons of numerous gigantic humanoids: a race of ancient giants. Brown quickly departed, both amazed and scared, and said nothing to anyone about the temple or its astounding contents for years. Rather curiously, however, decades later, and after having become overwhelmingly obsessed by the hidden realm and gone public with his story, Brown vanished on the eve of what was to be his ultimate quest to locate Aladdin's Cave of secrets. He was never seen again—just like those adventurous souls who claimed to have discovered similar, huge skeletons and a golden city below California's Death Valley in the 1920s and 1930s.

The next development of real significance in the strange saga of the Lemurians of Mount Shasta began in the 1930s when a man named Guy Warren Ballard, along with his wife, Edna, created what became known as the I AM Activity. Born in Iowa, and someone who served with the U.S. military during World War I and later worked as a mining engineer, Ballard told a story that was as fascinating as it was undeniably controversial. As someone whose life and belief systems were steeped in both occult teachings and theosophy, Ballard claimed that while hiking on Mount Shasta in 1930, he encountered the Count of Saint Germain, an 18th century alchemist who had supposedly uncovered the secrets of immortality. The count was variously described as being the Wandering Jew who taunted Jesus Christ on the way to the crucifixion; the son of Francis II Rakoczi, a prince of Transylvania; or the illegitimate son of the widow of Charles II of Spain, Maria Anna of Pfalz-Neuburg. Or, maybe all of them! At the very time of his most fortunate encounter, Ballard was on the mountain looking for what was described as an esoteric brotherhood, possibly an offshoot of the very same brotherhood that guarded the Tibetan *Book of Dzyan* as described by Helen Blavatsky, which only made matters even weirder.

Count of St. Germain: An enigmatic visitor to Mount Shasta
(copyright Nicolas Thomas, 1781)

It was during this experience on Mount Shasta that the enigmatic count reeled off to Ballard countless data on the future, positive role the United States would play in ushering in a new era for the people of Earth, as well as his personal knowledge of so-called Ascended Masters. The latter, the I AM Activity came to solidly accept, were once human people of both historical renown and major influence, including Jesus Christ and Maitreya. After their physical deaths, Ballard told his followers (who, by the dawning of the 1940s, were in excess of a highly impressive

one million) the Ascended Masters existed in supernatural form, but would impart words of deep wisdom to certain people on Earth who had significant roles to play in the Earth's future, including, of course, Guy and Edna Ballard. And that Ballard claimed loudly to have been the re-embodiment of George Washington only added further fuel to the controversial fire that forever seemed to surround him.

There was, needless to say, a great deal of debate concerning the I AM Activity and the Ballard family. Many within the local media of the day considered the whole thing to be one big scam designed to ensure the pair a great deal of money from gullible souls willing to donate their hard earned wages and savings to the curious cause. And that many of the original members of the group were also members of a near-fascist organization called the Silver Legion added even more to the debate. The Silver Legion—whose members went by the title of Silver Shirts— was established in 1933 by William Dudley Pelley, a racist, anti-Semitic character who had a deep admiration for Adolf Hitler and spiritualism. Guy Ballard, then, most certainly moved in controversial circles, and not all of them were to be found on the slopes of Mount Shasta. And the controversy continued.

In 1942, three years after Guy Ballard's death, Edna and their son, Donald, were charged with 18 counts of mail fraud, as a result of the unproved data contained in a variety of their books and pamphlets relative to Ascended Masters, Lemuria, Mount Shasta, and much more of an interconnected nature. And although the pair was convicted on each count, in what turned out to be a landmark case when it came to what could or could not be said or published in the name of religion without offering any form of evidence in support of such claims, the convictions were finally, and somewhat dramatically, overturned. Demonstrating the allure of Ballard's teachings, more than 80 years after his alleged encounter with the Count of Saint Germain on Mount Shasta, devotees of his movement continue to hold an annual event on the mountain—called the *I AM Come!* pageant—which gives praise to the life and teachings of Jesus Christ. Guy Ballard still looms large at Mount Shasta, long after his physical passing.

Like so many of the places we have examined in the pages of this book so far, Mount Shasta can also claim its very own Bigfoot. Its wild antics hit the local media on September 9, 1976, only a few days after the foul-smelling thing was seen near Cascade Gulch, which is located on the lower slopes of the legendary mount. The man that had the misfortune to cross paths with the monster was a logger from the town of Salmon: Virgil Larson.

In a subsequent interview with Sergeant Walt Bullington of the local police, the then 47-year-old Larson explained how a few days earlier, at around 8:30 a.m., he and a colleague, Pat Conway (both of the Columbia Helicopter Company) carefully negotiated the treacherous slope to their place of work, having left their truck at a parking area adjacent to the road. It was while they were getting their breath back at the base of the hilly area, that something occurred to Larson he most certainly was not anticipating in the slightest.

After a couple of minutes of taking a rest, Larsen's attention turned to the sound of loud, thumping footsteps coming down the hill. For a few moments he could see no one, but quite naturally assumed it was yet another colleague from the U.S. Forest Service. Finally, at a distance of around 50 feet, Larsen could now see what, at first, looked like a darkly dressed man descending along a crude pathway through the trees that the logging company had created.

With thick bushes and trees dominating the entire scene, however, Larsen could only get the barest glimpses of the figure as it made its lumbering way down the hill; so, he called out, wishing the character a good day. Bigfoot, evidently, is hardly one enamored by early-morning, genial chatter. The dark form suddenly stopped, briefly turned its head in Larson's direction, then began walking again, at a noticeably increased speed—all without any form of reply to Larsen's greeting. Then, when the thing was barely 15 feet away and no longer largely obliterated from view by the dense foliage, Larsen was at last able to see the enigmatic visitor in its fullest form. It was at this point that Larsen's mind became flooded by fear and panic: There was no man in his midst, after all. It was a 7-and-a-half-foot, bulky, black-hair-covered monstrosity that stunk like rotting meat. Having the disturbing impression that the creature was possibly sizing him up—whether as foe, food, or even both—Larsen didn't wait around to get a better look and very wisely fled the area at high speed.

Having raced to where Pat Conway was also taking a break before beginning the day's activities, Larsen breathlessly related to his amazed partner what he had just seen. Thirty minutes later, and armed with a couple of thick tree limbs for protection, the pair tentatively returned to the area and checked out the site. The creature was gone, but the terrible odor was still very much hanging around, and strange and indistinct tracks dominated the forest floor. It was now time, both men concluded, to bring in the sheriff.

Three Forest Service employees, Don Wopschal, Bob Gray, and Rex Lebow, soon arrived with Sergeant Bullington. Interestingly, Larsen's encounter was taken most seriously by officialdom, which surely begs the inevitable and thought-provoking question of: Was the seriousness prompted by other, earlier Bigfoot encounters in the area that had caught the attention of concerned authorities? Whatever the answer to that potentially important question, the positive response by the sheriff's office did not stop the authorities from ultimately trying to downplay the affair. A somewhat condescending suggestion was made that perhaps Larsen had been frightened by nothing stranger than a long-haired environmentalist who had a problem with loggers chopping down the old, mighty trees of Mount Shasta. Neither Larsen nor his wife was in any fashion satisfied by such a bizarre and unlikely theory. Larsen remained in a state of emotional turmoil for a number of days, and his wife stated that her husband was a man with three decades of experience working in the woods and one who had been frightened witless by his encounter. Mount Shasta had just become even weirder, if such a thing was even conceivably possible.

Finally, it may not be without some significance that also contained in the huge Cascade Range is Mount Rainier. It was there, on June 24, 1947, that a pilot named Kenneth Arnold witnessed a veritable armada of strange, aerial vehicles that practically singlehandedly ushered in the era of the flying saucer. Mountains of mystery, indeed.

Had enough of the dizzying heights of Mount Shasta? Let's hope so, as now it's time for a complete change of scenery. From seeking out enigmas on high, we're off to a mysterious and unsettling underworld.

18

New York City Subway, New York, USA

A late-night trip on the New York City subway, which opened its doors to the world in 1904 and is now home to 842 miles of track and 468 stations, might not be the safest of excursions. But, we're not talking about muggers and murderers. No, there are far more dangerous things said to be lurking in those old tunnels, sewer systems, and platforms that wind and coil their collective way deep beneath the Big Apple.

Mimic is a 1997 movie that tells the spooky story of gigantic, man-sized cockroaches living deep within the maze-like bowels of the New York City subway, that cunningly disguise themselves as black-cloaked human beings by pulling their large, dark wings around them. They savagely feast upon the city's unfortunates, vagrants, and just about anyone and everyone else who has the bad luck to cross their cold hearted paths after the sun has set. And though there is—fortunately for us—no evidence at all to suggest that huge insects really are dining on the good folk of the city, the possibility that other wild beasts may be doing exactly that cannot be totally ruled out.

One of the most persistent stories concerning the New York City subway system is that it is home to a largely hidden population of giant alligators that feast on the hobos, the homeless, the late-night travelers, and just about anyone else that has the misfortune to get in their monstrous and marauding way. Yes, just about everyone knows, and loves, the engaging stories, but most are content to write off such tales as simply friend-of-a-friend yarns and modern-day folklore. But, they would be wrong.

Contrary to popular assumption that the tales have no truth to them, they most certainly do. Or, at least, some of them do. One just has to know where to look for the facts, and then separate them from the fiction and the rumor mill. And in one particular case, that means the pages of the *New York Times*. It's a little-known reality that back in February 1935 the *Times* reported on the discovery of an alligator in the sewers— a story that was actually verified. In an article titled "Alligator Found in Uptown Sewer: Youths Shoveling Snow See the Animal Churning in Icy Water," it was revealed how a group of teenagers, led by Salvatore Condoluci, caught and killed the 7-foot-long beast they had found below an open manhole cover on 123rd Street, near the Harlem River.

Teddy May, who, for more than 30 years, was Commissioner of Sewers in New York, said that he did not initially believe the stories about the alligators that first came to his attention in the 1930s. But as more and more accounts surfaced from his staff who claimed to have seen alligators swimming the underground waters of the city, he felt he at least needed to check things out for himself. On doing so, and to his utter amazement, he claimed to have spotted a number of just such creatures; not massive in size, but still a fairly respectable several feet in length.

It's also a reality that the New York City subway system has extensive sewer systems running below it. And, some have quietly whispered, it wouldn't be a stretch at all for some of those beasts to make their way up from the old sewers to the higher levels of the subway, and maybe even to some of the now-closed down tunnels and platforms, where they could contentedly munch to their heart's content on the local rat and feral dog and cat populations.

Possibly of relevance to such a story, is the slightly conspiratorial saga of a man named Mark Cherry, who claimed, back in the mid-1960s, to have been standing alone on the platform at the 149th Street Grand Concourse, located in the Bronx, when he was quickly ushered out by two police officers amid a warning that there had been a flooding at the station. According to Cherry, as he started to leave the station, he turned around and, to his shock, claimed to have seen four subway workers hauling the lifeless body of an alligator onto the platform, and two others carrying a body bag of the type generally used to contain a human corpse. But, this was no ordinary alligator: it was an albino. A true story or not, it's an undeniable reality that the darkness of the lower levels of the subway system would provide a great deal of protection for an albino—a creature whose lack of dark pigment would offer it no protection from the sun. And albinism in alligators, while rare, is certainly not unknown. As for human deaths on the subway, well, it would not be at all difficult to claim that the presumed person's death was the result of something far more down-to-earth than an alligator attack. For example, between January 2003 and May 2007, there were no less than 211 subway fatalities on the New York subway system: some by murder, others by suicide, accident, and sudden death from heart attacks and the like. Adding one more death to the list, and then cunningly disguising it as an ordinary event, may not have been so difficult a task to achieve.

What do you do when someone earnestly tells you they have seen a distinctly weird creature roaming around the New York Subway System *and* the fringes of New

Deep in the New York Subway system, man-eating creatures dwell (copyright C.J. Cornish, 1905)

York's Central Park? Well, you try and evaluate what the witness has
to say, and you then do your best to try and come to some meaningful
conclusion; which is what we are obliged to do in the following, very
odd affair. It was late one night in May 1997 when Jordan—an assistant manager at a certain hotel that overlooks the park—was exiting the
72nd Street station, which is located at 72nd Street and Central Park
West, and that, as its name suggests, forms the Western edge of Central
Park. Just after stepping off the train and preparing to exit the station for
a late night shift, Jordan was frozen in his tracks by the sight of a 3- to
4-foot-tall, dark-haired, bipedal animal that charged along the station
platform, took an almighty leap onto the tracks, and quickly vanished
into the shadow-filled tunnels. The beast was only in sight for a few seconds, but Jordan was sure that what he had seen was some type of ape.

Most bizarre of all, none of the other 20 or so passengers seemed
to have seen the mysterious critter, which ultimately led Jordan to conclude that, perhaps, he—and he alone—had encountered the ghost of
a long-dead ape, rather than a creature of a physical nature. But what
was it doing on the New York Subway System late on a Saturday night
in 1997? Jordan was stuck for an answer. And the story is made even
stranger by the fact that this was not Jordan's only encounter with such
a creature. He saw a similar one on a sunny weekday in either June or
July 1997 as he was strolling through the park, not too far from the 72nd
Street station.

All was normal until, as he approached one particularly tree- and
bush-shrouded area, Jordan was shocked to the core when, out of nowhere, an unknown animal burst wildly through the foliage. He claimed
that the creature was man-like in shape and covered in hair of a distinctly
rusty color, rather than brown, which had been the case in the first
encounter—but, unlike the towering Bigfoot of the west-coast, was, just
like the one he had seen on the subway platform, just a tad more than 3
feet in height. "Little Foot" might have been a far better term to use in
this particular case.

Jordan could only watch with a mixture of shock and awe as the diminutive man-beast charged across the path in front of him at a distance
of about 20 feet, came to a screeching halt for a couple of seconds to
stare intently into his eyes, and then headed off at high speed again,

before finally vanishing beneath a small bridge inside the perimeter of the park. Whether provoked by the presence of a pair of spectral beasts—as he ultimately came to believe—or somebody's pet monkeys wildly on the loose, Jordan's story is just one of those very odd, fringe cases that seem to really perplex those of us who dare to dig into the world of monsters and strange creatures.

Although regular sightings of ghosts on the New York City subway are not as prevalent as they are in some of the Big Apple's old and his-toric buildings—such as the *Dakota*, an apartment building in which the Beatles' John Lennon lived until his murder in December 1980, (and who is rumored to haunt the 19th-century building), and the *Algonquin Hotel*, where the ghost of Harpo Marx is said to regularly frequent—they are most certainly not unknown.

Mabel Tanner claimed just such an encounter in 1937 and, in 1949 shared her story with a man named Raymond A. Palmer, the co-founder of *Fate* magazine and the editor of *Amazing Stories*. In Tanner's case, the location of her spooky subway encounter was the Franklin Avenue station in Brooklyn. According to the story told to Palmer, Tanner was entering the station when her attention was caught by the sight of a skinny and unkempt man dressed in the shabby uniform of a Confed-erate soldier of the American Civil War. Thinking that he must surely have been someone on his way to a costume party, Tanner smiled, and turned as the man passed by her in silence and failed to acknowledge her smile. It was Tanner's action that led her to realize the man was no mere partygoer. On turning her head, barely a second after the curiously dressed man went by, Tanner was overcome by fear when the strange character was nowhere to be seen. He had, quite literally, vanished into oblivion.

This particular case is a strange one. Ghosts, for the most part, are generally said to be associated with places they were familiar with in their physical lives. Yet, the Civil War was over long before the New York Subway system was even built. But, one might say that such a strange case is highly appropriate for an underground domain filled with man-eating alligators, and a dwarfish Bigfoot. Strange attracts strange, it seems very fair to say!

And you know what else attracts strange? Cemeteries, that's what. We've seen how such a place in central England is the lair of a werewolf. But what about a Mexican graveyard that can claim to play host to its very own vampire?

19

Panteon de Belen, Guadalajara, Mexico

A cemetery in Guadalajara, Mexico, that is noted for its highly decorative architecture, pillared buildings, elegant tombs and spacious, tree-enveloped grounds, Panteon de Belen was built in 1848 and closed its doors four years before the dawning of the 20th century. But, that hasn't stopped its residents from being highly active—which is somewhat notable because each and every one of them is, of course, quite dead! Not only that: Panteon de Belen can boast of being home to more ghosts, ghouls, and fiends of the night than pretty much any other cemetery in Mexico. That same body of supernatural entities includes just about everything from pirates to bloodthirsty, undead vampires, and spectral hounds to a ghostly, shrieking nun. And such is the interest and fascination in the specters of Panteon de Belen, that guided tours of the cemetery have become incredibly popular, and particularly so—and certainly most appropriately—during the course of the Mexican holiday of November 1–2: Day of the Dead. And, now, you shall see exactly why.

Without doubt one of the most macabre of all the many tales of terror attached to the cemetery is that of its very own, bloodthirsty monster of the night. So the story goes, back in the 19th century and to their eternal horror, people began finding the blood-drained corpses of numerous animals in the immediate vicinity of the old tombs. Bodies were also discovered torn apart and strewn around yards, on streets (particularly on Nardo Street, which is located only a few blocks from the graveyard), in nearby woods, and just about anywhere and everywhere else in the area. The savage nature of the attacks, coupled with the massive blood loss inevitably pointed to one thing and one thing only: Guadalajara was home to a rampaging and souless vampire. And when the predatory, undead monster suddenly turned its attentions to the children that lived in the immediate vicinity of Panteon de Belen, crazed hysteria truly broke out en masse. Just like in those old black and white monster movies of the 1930s and 1940s, frightened locals locked themselves behind closed doors at night, hung crosses outside their homes, and lived in deep fear of the cold-hearted killer now widely believed to be lurking among them.

The time eventually came, however, when enough was enough and a plan of action was put into place: a band of men, including a number of whom had lost children to the beast, were determined to put an end to the reign of terror that had crippled and blighted their lives. Suspecting that because many of the killings—of both children and animals—occurred in and around the cemetery, the wisest approach was to secretly stake out the old, cold graves by night and confront and kill the marauding monster. It was a plan that actually worked.

By the light of nothing but a full moon, the black-garbed, pale-faced fiend was cornered in the shadows of the cemetery, in the early hours of one particular morning, while greedily feasting upon the corpse of a newly slaughtered young girl. The outraged villagers wasted no time and lunged hard and fast at the undead thing. It took half a dozen men to pin the snarling, shrieking creature to the ground, but their actions paid off: one of the group, armed with the proverbial wooden stake, thrust it deep into the vampire's chest, ensuring its reign of terror came to a bloody and decisive end. A variation on the story suggests that, rather than having been confronted in the heart of Panteon de Belen itself, the vampire was spied prowling the shadowy streets in search of food, and was stealthily followed by the men to its abode—an innocuous-looking, small apartment on Nardo Street—where swift, cold justice was rapidly and decisively dished out.

That was not the end of the story—or stories—however. On the following morning, the body of the nightmarish figure was quickly buried in the grounds of the cemetery and covered in concrete, with the stake left firmly in place, deep in its black heart. Several months later, however, distinct cracks started to develop in the thick slab. A cold chill swept throughout the folk of the area. Was the vampire slowly forcing its way out of its concrete prison, as many initially feared was exactly what was going on? No. It was actually the roots of a tree that, legend says, sprouted from the wooden stake that had brought the reign of terror to a shuddering end. But this was no normal tree. Local folklore says that, even today, cutting the bark results in human blood, rather than sap, seeping from its now fully grown form. Others claim that the tortured faces of the victims of the monster can be seen imprinted in the branches and trunk of the tree. And, fearful that, if it should one day die, the vampire will be unleashed upon the townsfolk to once again embark on a deadly killing spree. Even to this very day, the tree is devotedly cared for, fed and watered, albeit from a perspective of sheer terror rather than love.

There can surely be very few people reading this book who have not at least heard of the legendary Mothman of Point Pleasant, West Virginia, that so terrorized the town and its surrounding areas between November 1966 and December 1967. The enigmatic exploits of this glowing eyed, gargoyle-like beast were chronicled in *The Mothman Prophecies*, the 2002 hit movie starring Richard Gere that was so named after the monumentally mysterious and entertaining book of the same title written by the Mothman authority, John Keel.

It might justifiably be said that, in March 2008, the Mothman headed for pastures new—in Panteon de Belen. The witness, Blanca Ramirez, was on vacation in Guadalajara, and had heard a legend that, as a fan of all things of a pirate-based nature, fascinated her. Local storytellers say that back in the late 1700s an infamous swashbuckler of the seas whose daily ritual, for years, had been to plunder and steal gold, silver, and all manner of riches and bounty from just about anyone and everyone else sailing the oceans, finally retired to the city, and spent some of his vast wealth on a lavish home near the cemetery. His time, however, was short. It wasn't long at all before the old man went from being a neighbor to a resident of Panteon de Belen and took to the grave with him the secret of where he stashed the remainder of his priceless plunder. But, for those would-be treasure hunters out there, Guadalajara lore says that if you visit the cemetery at midnight, light a candle, and pray that his soul will be free of punishment and torment for the actions in his physical life, the old man of the sea will appear before you and whisper in your ear the secret location of his priceless booty. Unfortunately, so the tale also goes, within minutes, the priceless information will forever fade from your mind and you will always be cursed with the knowledge that you came so close to having all your money worries solved in an instant.

A ghostly pirate walks the old cemetery of Panteon de Belen (copyright Jean Leon Gerome Ferris, 1920)

One suspects, however, that Blanca Ramirez got far more than she ever bargained for when she visited the cemetery in search of the paranormal pirate. According to Ramirez, while walking around the legendary tree of the vampire, she caught brief sight of a hideous figure gliding overhead at a perilously low level. It was a large, dark-colored, winged man whose glowing red eyes fixed firmly and icily on Ramirez for what was only an instant, but felt like a lifetime. Paralyzed with fear, she could do nothing but stare in a state of shock and terror as the beast suddenly soared into the sky at a phenomenally rapid rate and vanished into the thick, swirling clouds that hung broodingly over the length and breadth of the sinister cemetery.

Also of a paranormal, animalistic nature are the ghostly hounds that guard and roam around a tomb in the cemetery known as the Man of the Dogs. The curious name comes from the saga of an old character who lived on the streets of Guadalajara in the late 1800s and who, as a devoted lover of animals, cared for many of the stray dogs that lived on the old streets. He was a harmless beggar, one who had fallen upon hard times after developing a catastrophic gambling habit. Most people in the area took pity on the man by providing him with the occasional bit of money, food, and shelter. Not everyone was quite so charitable, however. Late one fateful night, the man was subjected to a vicious beating by a gang of drunken thugs. It quickly led to his death, but he did not stay down for long.

On the following night, the man's spectral form was seen by the terrified customers of a local bar that he frequented whenever there was sufficient pennies in-hand to purchase a cold, satisfying drink. And hot on his ghostly trail, as he glided silently through the bar, were his faithful hounds, still with him in his death. When the ghostly image faded into nothingness as it passed through a solid wall on the far side of the bar and with a mournful look on its face, a realization quickly developed that the man, whose body had been simply buried on the outskirts of town in nothing more than a dirty, dusty old stretch of wilderness, should be given a decent and respectable funeral in the cemetery—which he duly was—lest he remain a restless and roaming spirit until the very end of time.

The dogs that he so cared for were still not willing to leave their master and, while they wandered and played in the streets of Guadalajara by day, come sunset, they dutifully made their way to the cemetery and their dens around the grave of the old man. And, today, if you visit Panteon de Belen after darkness has set in, and you hear the woeful, eerie howling of a pack of dogs, it may not be an ordinary pack. It might just be the beggar's canine friends who, having also long departed this plane, now follow him as much in the afterlife as they did in the physical world. And from howling hounds we turn our attentions to a horrific, shrieking nun.

Her identity may not be known, but none who encounter the unholy creature will ever likely forget the experience. She is a gaunt, pale-faced old hag, with evil, penetrating eyes and long, bony fingers that extend from equally bony hands. And she walks the cemetery dressed in an outfit of a 19th-century nun. But this nun is not the sort that offers spiritual help, guidance, or religious teachings, however. She is a tormented and tormenting character that takes a great deal of vicious delight in bringing grave misfortune to those she deems worthy of her heartless wrath.

Should you find yourself in the wrong place at the wrong time and the nun appears before you, never, ever look into the depths of her fiery eyes. Doing so will ensure that all of your innermost secrets will instantly become hers. And if you have wronged someone in your life, not only will she know it, but she will cast down the same punishment to you that you once delivered. Some might say that's fair enough: she is merely dishing out a harsh sentence to those who have lived corrupt and evil lives. True, except for one thing: Depending on her mood, the nightmarish nun is not averse to targeting the good, the kind, and the selfless, too, generally with what amounts to a long-running bout of bad luck, ill-health, and misfortune.

Was the woman, as some residents of Guadalajara suggest, a sad figure that turned her back on the outside world as a teenager, and became a nun after being callously discarded by her older lover? And if so, has that ever-growing sadness and resentment, even in death, now reached a crazed level where everyone she encounters is ripe for her wild fury and bitterness? Keep those questions carefully in mind if, while taking a walk around Panteon de Belen, you encounter what looks like an elderly nun out for a pleasant stroll in the grounds of the cemetery. Make sure you do one other thing, too: run for both your life and soul. And you may want to do exactly the same thing should you stumble across the cemetery's resident vampire, ghostly beggar, spectral dogs, and Mothman, too!

Probably the only thing of a weird nature that has not been seen at Panteon de Belen is a spacecraft from the stars and its crew of bug-eyed aliens. But, don't worry, if the old cemetery can't help us in the E.T. stakes, then a spooky old forest near the east coast of England most certainly can.

20

Rendlesham Forest, Suffolk, England

Imagine the scene: It's late on a chilled, winter's night and the witching hour is looming perilously close. Your high-pressure job takes you out of town on a regular basis, and right now, after a hard week spent on the road, you just want to get home to your spouse and the comfort of your own bed. But before you can do both, you are forced to concentrate on driving through the winding, tree-shrouded roads of large, ancient woodland. Your eyes are tired, the light is poor, and mysterious shadows dominate your field of view. And, little do you know it, but there's something else on the road, too.

As you negotiate a sharp bend—a bend you have traveled on probably hundreds of occasions and one which is particularly dense with tree cover—you slow down and turn on your high beams to help illuminate the blackness that beckons. Suddenly, your eyes become hypnotized by something incredible on the right-side of the road. You hit the brakes hard and you sit, astonished and wide of mouth, never giving even a single thought to the possibility that another vehicle may slam into you from behind. Your mind is utterly elsewhere. And it's not surprising.

Glaring at you in menacing fashion, and sporting what appears to be a pair of large, glowing, yellow eyes, is a huge black cat. No, it's not just someone's spoiled, overfed pet. Rather, it's just about the closest thing you can think of to a fully grown, menacing puma. Its penetrating eyes bore into yours, it changes its stance to one of attack, and, while gripping the steering wheel and holding your breath, as if your very life depended on it, you try to prepare for the absolute, very worst. Fortunately, the worst does not come.

Without warning, the beast's head quickly turns. It races across the road, into the safety and camouflage of the trees, and is gone. You sit there, for a few minutes, trying desperately to get your breath back, and fighting off the rising panic that threatens to overwhelm you. Finally, the shaking in your hands begins to fade, as does the adrenaline-driven dizziness that hit you when overwhelming fear set in. It's then you realize the potentially life-threatening fact that your car sits in the middle of a dark road late at night. That practically no one is likely to be out, at this hour, on this very stretch is probably the only thing that has saved you from becoming the victim of a very nasty, and potentially fatal, accident.

You floor the accelerator, race home, and relate the details of the amazing experience to your spouse—who you have roused from slumber, an action prompted by a high degree of both excitement and fear. He or she listens carefully, and after having done so, the two of you come to a stark and sensational realization: You are one of the ever-growing number of people in the British Isles who has had a close encounter with a large, exotic, and predatory cat of a type that simply should not exist in Britain, and which the government says are merely the stuff of nightmare, mistaken identity, and hoaxing. But now, you know better—much better, in fact. Although, given the gut-wrenching experience you have just suffered, you earnestly wish you did not.

The story above is not fiction. It occurred in 1977 to a man named Jimmy Freeman. And the forest in question is no normal forest. It's an area that has been a veritable hotbed of supernatural strangeness for centuries. Nevermind just big cats, the forest can claim to be the domain of a strange Bigfoot-like creature known as the Shug Monkey. Sightings of ghostly entities abound. Fiery-eyed devil-dogs, provoking distinct imagery of *The Hound of the Baskervilles*, roam the woods. And, in December 1980, this very same locale was the setting for Britain's most infamous of all UFO encounters.

Adjacent to Rendlesham Forest, Royal Air Force Bentwaters is the domain of UFOs and the spectral East End Charlie (copyright Nick Redfern)

Its name is Rendlesham Forest, a 1,500 hectare of picturesque woods that is located on coastal heath land in the county of Suffolk, England— which played an integral role in the Roman invasion of the nation in AD 43—and near the ancient village of Butley, whose origins date back to the 1100s, and Ipswich, a town that began to take shape in Anglo-Saxon times, during the 7th and 8th centuries AD. It's amid this backdrop of history that one of England's weirdest of all places came to fruition.

Over the course of three amazing nights in the latter part of December 1980—specifically December 26 to 28—a series of sensational, otherworld encounters reportedly occurred deep in the heart of Rendlesham Forest. That the events in question involved a contingent of U.S. military personnel stationed at a *very* nearby British Royal Air Force installation called Bentwaters, and were reportedly the subject of deep and intense secrecy and cover-up, has led to claims that the affair in question amounts to a British equivalent of the Roswell, New Mexico, event of July 1947. Based on what you will now learn, those same claims may well be far more than justified.

Incredible on-the-record testimony from U.S. Air Force operatives tells of the landing in the woods of a craft from another world—a small, triangular-shaped UFO—of sightings of strange, ethereal, alien-like entities exiting that same craft, of the object tracked on radar, of elevated radiation readings recorded in the forest, and of a massive cover-up of the affair quickly put into place and carefully managed by concerned government officials of both Britain and the United States.

And, the evidence for some sort of extraordinary event having occurred is near-overwhelming and undeniable. Colonel Charles Halt of the U.S. Air Force, and one of the key witnesses to the events in Rendlesham Forest, prepared a memorandum for the British Ministry of Defense that detailed the amazing body of UFO activity at Rendlesham Forest in the final days of 1980. In Halt's own words to the MoD:

> …a red sun-like light was seen through the trees. It moved about and pulsed. At one point it appeared to throw off glowing particles and then broke into five separate white objects and then disappeared. Immediately thereafter, three star-like objects were noticed in the sky…the object to the south was visible for two or three hours and beamed down a stream of light from time to time. (Halt, 1980)

Strange lights, pulsating objects, and star-like craft beaming lights to the ground are, collectively, one thing. But, it's here that we have to turn to an even weirder event that occurred deep within the woods two nights later.

Darkness had fallen when a number of U.S. Air Force personnel were ordered to make their way through the thick trees, to a clearing that was blanketed by fog. But this was no normal fog. After all, how often do you get to see a fog that *glows*? On top of that, dozens of military

personnel were swarming around, clearly anticipating the arrival of...
something. As the amazed airmen watched, a tiny ball of red, glowing
light suddenly appeared out of nowhere, and flew toward the heart of the
eerie fog at high speed. Without any warning whatsoever, the entire area
was lit up by what seemed to be a multitude of camera flashes going off
simultaneously. The red ball of light was gone, and in its place was a
strange-looking craft, one that was pyramid-shaped and seemingly me-
tallic in nature.

Utterly stunned, the group could only stand in awe as a large ball of
light displaying alternating colors of blue and gold exited the UFO and
floated in their direction. But, more significant than the ball was what it
contained: three small, humanoid entities, with large heads and cat-like
eyes, sporting silver colored suits. *Aliens had just landed in Rendlesham
Forest*. After a tense few moments during which some sort of telepathic
communication between a senior military officer and one of the entities
reportedly took place, all of the men were ordered to carefully back
away, return to their vehicles, exit the woods, and head back to Royal
Air Force Bentwaters. What had begun on December 26 with the sighting of weird lights in the sky had ended on December 28 with a visita-
tion by beings from another world.

Thus was born the Rendlesham Forest UFO incident, one that is
seemingly destined never to go away. Indeed, in the three decades-plus
since the events of December 1980 occurred, more and more claims of a
truly sensational nature have surfaced. Now-retired military operatives
tell of being drugged and hypnotized by Men in Black-types, concerned
by what the airmen had seen in the woods, and doing whatever was
deemed necessary to silence them. Others talked of highly classified
files, film footage, and photographs held by British and American
authorities, both said to be fearful of telling what they *really* know of
those mysterious nights in the forest. The UFO secrets of Rendlesham
Forest, it seems, are set to stay just about as dark, shadowy, and mysterious as the place itself.

Moving on from aliens, Larry Warren, who was a prime player in
the UFO encounters of December 1980, has stated that while he was
stationed at Royal Air Force Bentwaters, there was a great deal of talk in
the area of mysterious matters of a distinctly supernatural, paranormal,

and occult nature going on deep in Rendlesham Forest. There were, says Warren, stories of witches and druids undertaking ritualistic activity in the area after sunset. There was also the legend of what was known on Bentwaters as the ghostly Lady Without a Face. How the spectral woman came to lose her face is unknown. But she was said to ride an equally ghostly bicycle along a stretch of old road that connected Bentwaters with a nearby military base, Royal Air Force Woodbridge. And she was hardly the friendliest of ghosts. A wailing and shrieking specter, she seemed intent in scaring the life out of just about anyone and everyone who dared cross her path.

The most famous ghost of Rendlesham, however, was East End Charlie. According to Larry Warren, the rumor mill on base was that he was the ghost of a World War II-era Nazi pilot who was shot down while flying over the forest during what has become known as the Battle of Britain, which extended from July to October of 1940. So the legend went, Charlie actually managed to successfully crash-land his aircraft in one of the nearby fields, and made his escape into the woods. That is, until irate local folk, who had seen his German fighter plane plummet to the ground, caught up with him, and, in a fashion more akin to torch-wielding villagers in one of those 1930s *Frankenstein* movies, burned him alive on a hastily made, roaring bonfire.

Larry Warren says that, despite the fiery ending that befell the unknown pilot, he was said to have been a playful, rather than malevolent, character. Although, on one occasion, Warren recalls, East End Charlie supposedly sat on the hood of the base fire department's patrol vehicle and burned his handprints into the metal.

And, now, let's move on from ghosts to hairy wild men. That's right: a British Bigfoot.

It is deeply ironic that many of those who are skeptical of the notion that aliens landed in Rendlesham Forest in December 1980, suggest that the airmen who were involved in the affair were merely mistaken by the bright illumination from the nearby Orford Lighthouse, the powerful beam of which *can* be seen from the old base and the woods. Why, you may ask, the reason for the irony? Well, the old town of Orford itself is no stranger to mystery—monstrous mystery, as it happens.

Back in the 1100s, a man named Ralph (last name unknown, but first a monk and later an abbot at Coggershall, Essex, England) contributed significant amounts of text to a mighty tome titled *Chronicon Anglicanum*. In its pages, he described the remarkable capture in Orford of a primitive, caveman-like beast. So Ralph told it, it was during the reign of King Henry II extending from 1133 to 1189, and while Bartholomew de Glanville was in charge of a medieval castle, which still stands at Orford to this day, that a group of men out fishing in coastal waters caught far more than a few tasty fish in their nets. If the story told to, and then later by, Ralph was not an outrageous lie, myth, or tall tale, then the land and waters around Rendlesham Forest were populated by a truly strange and savage beast centuries ago.

The pages of *Chronicon Anglicanum* describe how the captured creature was very much like a man, except that his entire body was covered in thick hair, and he possessed a long, shaggy beard. We can gain a few more tantalizing words from Ralph's very own description, and also of what ultimately became of the legendary man-beast held at Orford Castle. Ralph faithfully noted in his account that the wild man eagerly ate whatever was brought to him, but if it was meat, and in raw form, the hairy thing would first press it hard between his hands until all the juice was gone before taking a bite. And trying to engage the wild man in conversation was seemingly a totally fruitless task, too. He would not talk, even when tortured and strung up by his ankles. And, said Ralph, the monster-man of Orford showed no understanding of the concept of religion or the nature and purpose of a church, and was far more content to remain in his den at the castle.

Ultimately, it seems, the wild man became tired of his new surroundings, and eventually fled. On one particular day, as Ralph told it, the wild man was permitted to go back into the sea from which he was originally taken, albeit surrounded on all sides by men with large nets, just in case he attempted to escape. As fate would have it, the hairy man did escape. After swimming in his old, familiar waters for a while, the creature suddenly made a break for freedom and vanished under the waves. He was never seen nor heard of again.

Rendlesham Forest, as well as the Suffolk locales of West Wratting and Balsham, is also said to be the home of a Bigfoot-type animal known for centuries as the Shug Monkey—*Shug* being a distortion of an old English word, *scucca*, which translates, somewhat ominously, as *demon*. Perhaps the descendents of the beast immortalized in *Chronicon Anglicanum* by Ralph of Coggershall continue to live on, lurking and surviving in the wilder and denser parts of Rendlesham Forest and its immediate surroundings; a disturbing thought, to say the least.

Then there are Rendlesham's devil dogs.

Bob Trubshaw, an authority on sightings of gigantic, fiery-eyed, black hounds that, for centuries, have haunted the old tracks, paths, waterways, and crossroads of Britain, says that they frequently forewarn of death and tragedy and are "part of a world-wide belief that dogs are sensitive to spirits and the approach of death, and keep watch over the dead and dying." And though the image that the phantom black dog of Rendlesham Forest creates is one of a deadly and devilish beast that prowled the area centuries ago, it is a little-known fact outside of students of the phenomenon that occasional sightings of these unsettling creatures surfaced until at least the 1980s (Trubshaw).

On a cold winter's afternoon in 1983, for example, the soon-to-be-married Paul and Jane Jennings were blissfully strolling through the woods of Rendlesham when they were terrified by the sudden manifestation in front of them of what Jane would describe succinctly as a big black dog. She elaborated that the pair had been walking along a pathway when, on rounding a bend, they came face-to-face with the phantom beast—something that prompted Jane to intriguingly conclude that the beast had somehow anticipated their presence and manifested accordingly.

Reportedly, the beast's head was clearly canine in appearance, albeit much larger than that of any normal dog. Yet, its body seemed to exhibit characteristics that were cat-like. For a brief and tense moment they stared at the creature, which, they recalled, seemed to have an eerily mournful expression upon its face.

Suddenly, the beast began to lose form, and took on ethereal and translucent appearance, before finally fading away into absolute nothingness amid a powerful odor eerily reminiscent of brimstone. The Jennings fled the woods, never to return. Thankfully, however, they were spared death and tragedy; unlike so many who have crossed paths with the infernal devil dog.

Sightings of strange phenomena in the woods continue. In the 2000s, for example, a mysterious and huge cat of the type seen by Jimmy Freeman back in 1977 returned to the area. It terrorized the likes of June Fooks, who saw the beast in her yard and that she described as being bigger than her Labrador. Anne Downing encountered a similar creature in Rendlesham Forest. According to Downing, it was while walking along a pathway with her daughter that she caught sight of a large black creature in the distance and whose stance suggested it was about to pounce on something. As mother and daughter tentatively edged closer, the creature fled into the undergrowth and was gone. Rendlesham Forest: truly, an ongoing site of definitive, unearthly weirdness.

At this stage, I probably don't need to tell you that much the same can be said about our next port of call, but I will anyway. Brace yourself: We're on a hunt for trolls and elves in chilly Iceland.

21

Reykjavik, Iceland

The Republic of Iceland is a small, island country in the North Atlantic Ocean with a population of only a little more than 300,000. Its colorful and historic heritage extends back to AD 74 when a powerful Norse chieftain, Ingolfur Arnarson, landed on its shores and established a permanent foothold that grew and grew. And with a landscape dominated by huge glaciers, imposing mountains, the largest waterfall in Europe, still-active volcanoes, cold, flowing rivers, and powerful geysers, it's an undeniably atmospheric country. Iceland is bustling with supernatural activity and paranormal entities, and particularly so in and around the capital of Reykjavik. Top of the list are, without doubt, the land's legendary elves and trolls: the *hulte volk*, or *hidden people*.

Originally believed to have been ancient gods who held sway over issues relative to fertility and nature, the elves of Reykjavik are a curious bunch that, via folklore and legend, have become inextricably tied to other elemental entities such as fairies and goblins. They can be as helpful and friendly as they can be malevolent, and display distinct traits

159

of both teacher and tormentor. Preferring to spend their time in wells, forests, and springs, and not always diminutive in size (as most people might assume, given how elves have for so long been portrayed in folklore), they have an uneasy relationship with the people of the land. They are a highly unpredictable bunch, too. Though they will not hesitate to wreak unrelenting supernatural havoc if they feel they have been disrespected, they often display both incredible generosity and playfulness if the mood, and the person, takes them.

Snorri Sturluson, an Icelandic historian who lived from 1179 to 1241, was deeply familiar with such creatures and maintained there were several categories, including the Dokkalfar—or dark elves—and Ljosalfar—light elves. Sturluson said the light elves were more radiant than the sun, whereas the dark elves were darker than night. And that the former are said to live in a tranquil locale and the latter in dark, underground dwellings. Interestingly, many of the stories of Icelandic elves emanate from Hafnarfjordur, a small town just south of Reykjavik that is believed to be a place saturated by mystical energies and portals to other realms or dimensions of existence.

To demonstrate the sheer extent to which the people of Reykjavik, even today, fully believe in the existence of such creatures, studies undertaken by the University of Iceland's Faculty of Social Sciences in 2006 and 2007 revealed that whole swathes of the population were very open-minded on the matter of their undeniably widespread elf legends. And when a poll was taken in 2009, it showed that although around 50 percent of the populace felt that such creatures *might* exist, more than 10

Within the Icelandic culture, elves are far more than mere legend (copyright George Pearson, 1871) percent were absolutely *sure* of their reality. Even Iceland's Road Authority has, on more than several occasions, been forced to modify, or outright alter, its plans to build new roads and highways in areas of magical renown said to be inhabited by elves, for fear of incurring the malevolent wrath of the creatures.

The trolls of Rekjavik, are, without doubt, of equal significance and importance to the people of the nation's capital as are their elves. And just like elves, trolls have a particular liking for mountainous regions, cold and dark caves, and dark, shadowy woods. Today, the general and popular imagery of the troll is of a giant, man-eating creature that is big on muscles but short on brains; one that sports a head of long, shaggy hair and dresses in animal skins. This is most assuredly not always so, however. The trolls of Rekjavik are also described as being extremely human-like in appearance, and are creatures that can most often be identified by their predilection for avoiding human society and mainstream religion. But, there can be no doubt that it is the former category that dominates Reykjavik folklore.

The man-beasts were, in centuries long gone, notorious for their violent ways, bad tempers, and reputations for raiding isolated farms and homes in the wilds of Iceland in search of food, and, sometimes even a damsel or several to take as their wife, or even to heartily devour. Eating humans has never been beyond the average Icelandic troll. Or, beyond the male trolls, at least. The females are quite a different story. Longstanding legend in Reykjavik says that in the distant past, whereas the men-folk of their kind were violent killers and devourers of human beings, the women were not. Indeed, they had a particular thing for human men and would often cast magical spells to lure those that caught their eye to their lairs, and force them to live, and even mate, with them. Thus, over time, Iceland's trolls became less and less pure and more and more half-troll and half-human. The offspring, however, while looking very human in physical appearance, retained the supernatural abilities of the troll, such as magical enchantment.

Somewhat related to Reykjavik's trolls are its Joselveinar, which translates into English as yule lads or yule men. Today, they are the Icelandic equivalent of the smiling, gift-giving Santa Claus. But, they have a dark and disturbing history attached to them. In earlier centuries, the yule lads, said to have been the sons of an Icelandic ogress named Gryla, who lived high in the cold and rocky mountains of Iceland, became notorious for raiding lonely homesteads and villages in the vicinity of Reykjavik, just like the trolls of the land, and displaying homicidal tendencies whenever crossed by man. And their mother was, and still is, no better either. The Icelandic equivalent of the Bogeyman, Gryla is a murderous, hag-like creature with hooves instead of feet, 15 tails emanating from her lower back, and an eye protruding from the back of her skull. And Gryla strikes chilled fear in the hearts of the children of Reykjavik; which is hardly surprising because it is said that she has a great taste for their flesh, bones, and blood. Echoing this belief, the favorite dish of Gryla is a thick stew comprised of the body parts of youngsters who do not follow their parents' rules, which she heartily devours with her husband, Leppaluoi, in her strange abode: an area of volcanic caves and lava fields known as Dimmuborgir. It's an area, I might add, guarded by a large, fiendish cat of undeniably paranormal origins—the yule cat—that just like its master, Gryla, has a taste for the flesh of the young. The yule cat is not the only creature that has struck fear into the people of Reykjavik, however.

Over the course of several days in 1874, and only a short walk from the edges of the city, a strange beast was seen roaming the fringes of a nearby lake. The animal somewhat resembled a large, elongated dog, but possessed the long tail and neck that are absolute staple parts of the average lake-monster. That the animal fell into the latter category was made even more evident when, after prowling around the shore during the day, by evening it would take a flying leap into the waters and vanish into the murky depths, only very occasionally surfacing, as if, quite possibly, to take in a large gulp of air. Then, after less than a week, the sightings stopped—for a while.

By the following spring, the beast was back. And, by now, it had developed a foul temper and, by cover of darkness, stealthily and regularly left the confines of the lake to make its way to the nearby farms where it would feast voraciously upon the local sheep population. Angered and frightened farmers demanded swift action, and a local hunter was quickly enlisted to rid the area of the terrible thing. It was all to no avail, however. Eerily anticipating the presence and intent of the man, as he approached with gun in hand and while it swam near the shore, the creature plunged below with a mighty splash, never to be seen again. While Lars Thomas, an authority on lake-monster stories, says that the description of the creature suggests the legend might have been born out of nothing stranger than the antics of a seal, he concedes that the long neck and tail possibly suggest something very different, and leave the door open to something undeniably and truly monstrous.

Now we move to a certain, mysterious, Icelandic lake known as Lagarfljot, through which the River Lagarfljot flows and from which reports of both a Loch Ness Monster-style creature and a crashed UFO have surfaced. Notably, both stories have a tie to Reykjavik. As for the monster-serpent of the lake, its name is *Lagarfljotsormur*—or Iceland Worm Monster—and reports of its antics and appearances date back to 1345. Like Nessie of Scotland, it is a long-necked, humped beast, possessed of a powerful tail and large flippers that propel it swiftly through the cold waters.

Just like Scotland's most famous monster, too, the Icelandic equivalent has occasionally been seen basking on the shores, oblivious to, or uncaring about, the response of jaw-dropping astonishment it provokes in those who encounter it. Whereas Nessie is generally described as being anywhere from 15 to 50 feet in length, however, Lagarfljotsormur is *immense*, at around 300 feet, some even claim. So, what might the beast actually be: a surviving relic from the prehistoric age? Not according to the people of Iceland. They take a far more paranormal approach to the mystery.

Legend has it that the origins of the story of the monster can be found in the actions of a young girl originally from Reykjavik, but living in the area. One day, after having been given a gold ring by her mother, asked how she might best profit from it. Her mother's advice was odd: Place it under a lungworm (a parasitic creature that infects the lungs of its host). Despite the curious words of her mother, the girl the trusting girl did as she was told. She caught herself such a worm and placed it in a drawer in her bedroom with the ring placed carefully beneath it, which was a fatal mistake, to be sure. Only a few days later, and to the complete consternation of both mother and daughter, the worm grew at an immense rate, smashed its way out of the drawer, and caused chaos in the bedroom until it was overpowered and quickly thrown into the lake. Then, in the depths of the water, it grew, and grew, and grew, eventually causing mayhem and havoc when it realized that, by making brief excursions onto land, it could feast upon the farm animals of the area. And despite all attempts by a Reykjavik hunter to slaughter the beast, none were ever successful. It lived on, and, legend says, continues to do so. You may not wish to encounter Lagarfljotsormur up close and personal, however, as to do so is said to provoke bad luck and ill health—and perhaps even death for the unfortunate eyewitness.

Now to Iceland's crashed UFO, a case secretly investigated by the U.S. Air Force back in the 1950s. A two-page document, prepared by the 468th Counter-Intelligence Corps (CIC) detachment of the U.S. Air Force Office of Special Investigations (AFOSI), describes an intriguing event that occurred in the River Lagarfljot in August 1954. The paperwork in question, declassified under the terms of the Freedom of Information Act, and available for scrutiny at the National Archives, tells a notable story. And that the U.S. Air Force coordinated its investigation of the affair out of Reykjavik only makes things even more eye-opening.

According to the Air Force's files, shortly before 9 p.m. on the night of August 24, 1954, a fast-moving, low-flying, dark gray, cylindrical-shaped UFO was seen in the vicinity of Egilsstadir by an individual at Hjardabol, a farm located near the junction of the Lagarfljot and Jokula Rivers, in Northeastern Iceland. The event would probably have been dismissed, for lack of evidence, particularly because it took the witness a full week to summon up the courage to tell the authorities, were it not for one startling aspect of the story. The man in question, a farmer whose name is excised from the files, told the Air Force that as he watched the unknown craft on its flight-path, it suddenly lost speed and slammed into and violently bounced across a sand-bar on the Lagarfljot River, and quickly sank into the water.

Evidently greatly impressed by the words of the farmer, Icelandic and U.S. military personnel hastily set off from Reykjavik to the scene of all the potential alien action. And given what was potentially at stake—the possible recovery of a craft from another world—the search was extremely meticulous. It was September 11, 1954, when the team finally reached the exact point of impact, but, unfortunately, as the Air Force noted: "Between the time of the sighting, the Lagarfljot River had risen twice and washed over the sand-bar where the object reportedly landed, altering the size and shape of the sand-bar" (Counter-Intelligence Corps).

The military was far from dissuaded from pressing on, however. Upon satisfying themselves that they had reached the right spot, the Icelandic/American team brought in a trio of metal detectors in an effort to determine if they might assist in locating the object, or perhaps priceless fragments of it. It was an action that ended in failure, much to the deep frustration of all involved. But they were not quite done yet. Local divers were even enlisted—and sworn to secrecy in the process—to search for the device on the riverbed, but they too came up empty-handed.

There were two possibilities, the Air Force concluded: the UFO had not sunk to the bottom of the river, but was swept along by the running waters and was now much further away than suspected, or it was deeply buried in the bed of the river, something that would require considerable equipment to locate and recover it. Interestingly, although Air Force files exist (and have also been declassified into the public domain) showing that plans were initiated to carefully and completely search the entire river bed with sophisticated equipment, including portable cranes from Reykjavik, the files revealing the outcome of this action, rather predictably, have yet to see the light of day. Perhaps Icelandic and American military personnel really did secretly recover a ship from another galaxy back in 1954. Or, even more amazing and thought-provoking, perhaps it still remains buried, somewhere deep in the mud of the Lagarfljot River.

Now, from a little-known story of a crashed UFO in Iceland, to the absolute granddaddy of all such cosmic calamities: New Mexico, the desert, 1947. You've got it, my friends: *Roswell*...

22

Roswell, New Mexico, USA

In the summer of 1947, *something* significant and strange crashed to earth in the blisteringly hot and barren deserts of Lincoln County, New Mexico. Tales of a huge field of strange, super-strong debris, of a wrecked spacecraft from another world, and even of pulverized, dwarfish alien bodies having been found at the site proliferate and have done so for decades. The event in question has been the subject of a variety of books, official investigations undertaken by elements of both the government and the military, numerous television documentaries, intense media coverage and speculation, and has left in its wake a legacy of controversy and a web of intrigue that continue to reverberate more than 60 years later. That event has come to be known worldwide as the *Roswell Incident*.

It is a matter of recorded fact that in early July 1947, the then Roswell Army Air Force Base announced in a press-release that it had recovered the remains of what was termed a flying disc that had been found scattered across a wide area of the Foster Ranch by employee

William Ware Brazel. Intense media frenzy followed and was only brought to a swift and conclusive halt when the Roswell AAF hastily retracted its statement: the Flying Disc story was a huge mistake. Nothing more unusual than a weather balloon was retrieved, the press, and the people of Roswell, were assured. Today, rather intriguingly, the Air Force tells a very different story. The debris found at Roswell came not from a weather device or an alien craft, but from a top-secret balloon-based operation, code-named *Mogul,* designed to monitor Soviet nuclear tests. As for the claims of unusual-looking—or alien—bodies having been found at the site, they were, in reality, says the Air Force, simply crash-test dummies utilized in high-altitude parachute experiments.

Meanwhile, those within the UFO research community that champion the idea that something truly anomalous occurred at Roswell scoff at the ever-mutating assertions of the Pentagon and maintain that a conspiracy of cosmic proportions exists at the highest level to hide the truth of the affair, and its alien origins.

The city of Roswell—which was founded in the late 1800s by Nebraskan businessman Van C. Smith, and his partner, Aaron Wilburn—basks comfortably in the never-ending notoriety that the 1947 event provoked. And, financially speaking, its people have most assuredly benefited very well from whatever it really was that happened on that fateful day in early July 1947. Every year, tens of thousands of eager souls flock to Roswell, from all corners of the globe, to learn all about the legendary flying saucer crash. Far lesser-known, however, are the additional paranormal mysteries of Roswell, many of which have nothing at all to do with creatures of a world far, far away.

On a particular day back in 1936, a local woman—one who claimed the power of prophecy—predicted that doom and disaster were on the cosmic cards, and loudly proclaimed that the city of Roswell would be swallowed whole that very night when the ground beneath it would open up. Although some of Roswell's people were content to just laugh at her claims, others were not so confident and fled for the safety of higher ground on Six-Mile Hill, a ridge that forms the western horizon of Roswell. They may have been very wise to do so. Although the prophecy did not come to pass on that particular night, precisely a year after the woman made her prediction, Roswell was hit by a catastrophic flood.

Then there are the findings of a local man, John LeMay, who has collected numerous reports of seemingly paranormal and mysterious activity and places in the Roswell area, including the sighting of a Bigfoot outside of town; a mini-dinosaur on the loose; mysterious, bottomless lakes that swallow cars whole and spew them out in the Carlsbad Caverns; and out-of-place alligators that would be quite at home on the New York subway system. And then there's Roswell's army of ghosts.

For many years, Roswell's Victorian-era Chaves County courthouse served as the only place of execution for the most violent and cold-hearted criminals in the state of New Mexico. Death and the old building went together pretty much hand-in-glove and, for years, the ghostly cries of young children have been heard emanating, in eerie echoing style, from the shadowy basement. Were they, perhaps, the victims of some of those strung-up for their cold-hearted, terrible crimes?

The pecan orchards that dominate the area around Country Club Road, which were established in 1963 by an oilman named Olen Featherstone, are said to be the dwelling of yet another spectral child, a young boy who roams the streets and the fields, always crying and in a woeful, distressed state. Most curiously, his spectral form—which only appears on Sundays during the month of October and most often around the closest Sunday to Halloween—lacks any legs. Some suggest that the boy may have been the victim of a terrible accident, one in which he was violently torn apart and killed.

The city's Pueblo Auditorium, constructed in 1929 and where, on Valentine's Day, 1955, a then-unknown Elvis Presley performed, is also the home to the spirit of a child returned from the grave. He forever lurks around the balcony area, playfully enticing people to come to him, at which point he always enigmatically vanishes into the ether. And then there is the multitude of specters that haunt the city's New Mexico Military Institute (NMMI), which was established in 1891 by Joseph C. Lea, who chose Confederate colonel Robert S. Goss to head it. Somewhat appropriately, the NMMI can claim a near-army of specters. Each and every one of them originated with what was known as the Juliet troop, which was wiped out in the 1800s during a disastrous and calamitous firefight with Native Americans. The ethereal forms of the obliterated Juliet troop are still occasionally viewed in and around the institute today.

Roswell, New Mexico: home to far stranger things than just UFOs (copyright Nick Redfern)

Certainly, the most sensational of all the stories pertaining to Roswell's ghosts is the one that is directly linked to the legendary UFO crash, but in a highly peculiar fashion. Some suspect that the discarnate souls of alien entities killed in the violent fall from the skies still haunt the very building where they were said to have been secretly taken by the military in July 1947. At the time of the controversial incident, the building in question was an old, wooden one called the Roswell Army Air Field Hospital. By the early 1950s, the base had a new name, Walker Air Force Base. And with the name change, came another alteration: the hospital closed its doors. The cold, empty, and echoing hospital remained in definitive limbo until 1967, when it was finally torn down and replaced by a new brick building that, today, goes by the name of the New Mexico Rehabilitation Center (NMRC). But, even when they no longer exist, old buildings seemingly have a habit of ensuring they retain an icy and steely grip over the land upon which they once stood.

In 2004, Jim Marrs traveled to New Mexico, and specifically to the NMRC, where he was due to be filmed for a television documentary. It was while Marrs was speaking with Jacqueline Allen, the assistant to the NMRC's executive director, John Cooper that he learned that most of the staff was deeply wary of being in the second-floor corridors and rooms where, allegedly, a number of the alien bodies were systematically and quickly autopsied back in 1947. The reason for that same wariness, Allen told Marrs, was that incidents of a strange and unsettling nature had occurred there, time and again. His journalistic interest now piqued, Marrs pressed for more information. Footsteps could be heard, but with no discernible source. Lights would flash on and off. Elevator doors would open and close for no fathomable reason. And, just occasion-ally, the spectral form of a World War II pilot would be seen roaming the corridors, and who, more often than not, would give a genial wave or salute. That was nothing compared to the phantom alien presence, however.

Jacqueline Allen spoke of how, during one particular night shift in 1997, she was told by one of the nurses that a small, spectral alien-style entity had been seen standing at the end of the hallway on the second floor. One moment it was there, staring eerily at the nurse; the very next instant it was gone. A similar story came to Marrs' attention via Josie, an employee of the center who claimed to have witnessed quite possibly the very same entity on two occasions. Josie was adamant that what she encountered was an approximately 5-foot-tall, ethereal, specter-like being with a large, egg-shaped head and two enormous, black, oblong-shaped eyes. Interestingly, Josie said that on each occasion, she saw the apparitional alien, she experienced a distinct, but fortunately brief, feel-ing of bodily paralysis.

In November 2005, and in specific response to Jim Marrs' discoveries, a team consisting of me, author and ghost expert Joshua P. Warren, paranormal investigator Brian Irish, UFO hunter Ruben Uriarte, psy-chics Laura Lee and Karyn Reece, unsolved mysteries author Heidi Hollis, Native American Indian Richard Hernandez, and Jim Marrs flew to Roswell to investigate the claims of ghost aliens at the NMRC for a *Discovery Channel* television show called *X-Ops*. After speaking to the staff of the New Mexico Rehabilitation Center, and confirming their sto-ries as previously told to Marrs, we headed out to Hangar 84 at the old Roswell Army Air Field—the hangar reportedly being the place where the bodies were briefly held before being transferred to the hospital for autopsy and study. The purpose of our visit to the hangar: to conduct a midnight séance, one designed to invoke the presence of the alien dead.

On a cold night with a dominating, howling wind, we set up a large table replete with cloth and flickering candles, and settled down to see if the souls from the stars were prepared to put in an appearance for us.

And, just maybe, they did precisely that. As *Discovery's* camera crew began to film, Karyn Reece began her supernatural summoning—which coincided with the wind howling even more, and the walls of the old hangar creaking and groaning as if they were about to burst.

Without warning, one of the cameramen keeled over into a dead faint, and chaos and concern erupted. We were urged, however, to continue with the séance, while the man was carefully and quietly dragged to one side to recover. Attempts were made to contact the aliens, at which point the psychics reported visualizing bleak imagery of airborne calamity high above a sprawling, hot desert, of death and disaster, and of a tragic and tortured end for space-farers from a far away world. Members of our team, perhaps, had made psychic contact with the souls of extraterrestrials who appeared to be forever trapped in some sort of near-purgatory state in the heart of Roswell.

Then there came the veritable highlight of the night, although certainly none of us knew it until the film footage was finally viewed and studied. While the séance was in full swing, the camera team captured the jaw-dropping sight of what looked like a semi-transparent, hideous snake-like creature coiling just above our heads as we sat at the table, with our eyes closed and holding hands, focused on provoking ghostly, alien contact. As the footage revealed, the unholy beast circled its way around us while we sat, mercifully oblivious to its vile presence. Then, in an instant and as the footage demonstrated, the hideous thing was gone.

And there is one final matter worth mentioning: Although everyone on the shoot—cast, crew, producer, and director—was overwhelmingly pleased and enthusiastic about what had been achieved on that memorably supernatural November's eve in 2005, the *Discovery Channel* chose never to air the program. From 1947 to the present day, and from ghosts to aliens, some might say that conspiracies and Roswell continue to go together.

If all this gallivanting around the world has you downright breathless by now, not to worry: Our next paranormal place is only one state away from New Mexico. But, it's no less bizarre. It just might be even more so.

23

Sedona, Arizona, USA

Some 120 miles north of Phoenix, Arizona, in the northern Verde Valley, is Sedona, a small, tranquil city of barely 10,000 people that has become legendary in New Age circles for its enigmatic energies; vortexes; Native American legends of supernatural entities roaming the surrounding countryside; profound UFO encounters, and much more of a paranormal and strange nature. Sedona is also home to the famous Red Rocks, large and stunning formations of sandstone that glow an eerie and captivating red and orange when the sun both rises and sets, and which add even further to Sedona's reputation as a place of deep mystery and wonder. But, before we get to all of the above, let's begin with what just might be Sedona's strangest, and near-magical, inhabitants: the Rock People.

Although Sedona, as a city, was not founded until 1902, archaeological evidence in the form of ancient cave dwellings in the old canyons of town suggests a strong Native American presence in the area extending as far back as 9,000 BC. And within the old folklore of those same people, there existed the Wapeka, or, as they are more widely referred to today, the Rock People. Somewhat ethereal entities, the Rock People were said to be diminutive folk that secretly dwelled in underground caves and caverns hidden in the canyons. Lore suggests they possessed the uncanny ability to exist in both physical and spirit form, and to be at one moment visible and in another utterly invisible. And, just like the fairies, gnomes, and goblins of old England, the Rock People could be playful, helpful, and friendly, but, if disrespected or looked down upon, could rapidly turn downright malevolent, bent on cold-hearted, and sometimes even fatal, revenge. The Native American tribes of Sedona quickly and astutely recognized the wildly unpredictable nature and character of the Wapeka, and very wisely chose to form a positive relationship with them from earliest times, which resulted in bountiful harvests, good health, and an atmosphere of peacefulness and balance.

Possibly related to the Wapeka are the equally dwarfish Kakaka. Immortal beings that inhabit hollowed out areas of the surrounding mountains, they existed long before humankind came on the scene—even in its most primitive and primal form—and, for the most part, only prefer to surface from their darkened lairs long after sunset and when utter blackness has fallen upon Sedona. Just occasionally, if you happen to be in the right place at the right time, you might be lucky enough—or *unlucky* enough—to hear their chilling wailing and howling carried across the Red Rocks and the canyons by a powerful, biting wind.

Biologist Lyall Watson has noted that: "Navigation is bedeviled by the fact that the earth's magnetic field is riddled with local deviations and irregularities. These faults have been very carefully plotted and the most persistent of them have become quite notorious." Interestingly, Watson identified one such fault as existing near to Prescott, Arizona. It so happens that the distance from Prescott to Sedona is barely 30 miles (Sutphen).

But, what might such "faults" actually be? Dick Sutphen, an expert on the lore, legend, and mysteries of Sedona, says: "What Watson is describing is a vortex—a positive or negative 'power spot'—where a great concentration of energy emits from the earth. Positive vortexes expand and perpetuate energy; negative vortexes dissipate energy" (Ibid.).

It may very well be the case that Jeannie Howard encountered just such a vortex back in 1988, while walking around Sedona's Boynton Canyon, which, Sedona authority Tom Dongo notes, is home to seven major concentrations of energy. Howard had a passion for archaeology and history, particularly that of the Native American people. She maintains that while hiking through the canyon one morning in the fall of 1988, she suddenly, and for no particular reason, began to feel uneasy, clammy, cold, and dizzy. Most ominous of all, she developed the distinct feeling of being watched by hidden, sinister figures that wished her distinct ill will. This feeling was elevated to extreme levels when, Howard added, she suddenly saw, 20 feet in front of her, a small, humanoid creature bound across the pathway, while giving her a deeply unsettling, malevolent frown as it did so. The entity, said Howard, was 3 feet tall, had skin of a pale yellow color, a very human-looking face, a head of long hair tied back in a ponytail, and was naked. Not surprisingly, Howard gave out a loud scream, cried for help, and was rooted to the spot for about two minutes, frozen with fear.

Finally, Howard chose to tentatively move forward, wondering if she might have the opportunity to see the curious little man again, but she did not. Howard had barely moved 30 or 40 feet along the slope when she came to a sudden halt. And it was not a halt by choice, either. It was as if, Howard explained, she had walked headlong into an invisible door, but one that, rather than being solid, was more cushion-like, as she worded it. By that, she meant it was possible to push on the invisible barrier, and even to slightly move it backward and affect its shape, but no matter how hard she tried, she could not get passed it or through it. After a few more moments, Howard's mind became flooded by panic and she ran, hysterically, for the safety of her car, followed by a high-speed drive back to her motel room in town. Given that, by her own, somewhat sheepish admission, Howard's intention was to find and take home with her (in other words, steal) archaeological evidence of the old Native American presence in the area, one has to wonder if what she first encountered was an enraged Kakaka or Wapeka, followed by one of Dick Sutphen's energy-manipulating vortexes ensuring that Howard would be thwarted in her attempts to plunder the historical and magical area for personal gain.

Strange energies and unearthly entities abound at Sedona, Arizona (copyright Nick Redfern)

Moving on from the wee folk and invisible barriers, let us now focus on the one other paranormal puzzle that is evident around Sedona: UFOs. Fantastically wide and varied encounters with the denizens of unidentified aerial craft continually dominate the skies and landscape of Sedona. But, one that really stands out in the weird stakes occurred back in the summer of 1947, the details of which can be found in a formerly classified FBI file, now made available via the terms of the Freedom of Information Act.

According to the document of August 17, 1947—titled "Flying Disk, Sedona, Arizona"—the witness (whose name has been blacked-out in the copy of the file declassified by FBI censors) was a former World War II pilot who, after the hostilities came to an end in 1945, spent the next 18 months working as a crop-duster in West Texas, before moving to Sedona, and securing employment in nearby Prescott. It was while driving home late one week night (the man told the local sheriff's office, who, in turn, contacted both the military and the FBI) that he caught sight of a large ball of blue light hanging low in the sky over one of the canyons of Sedona.

Naturally curious, the man brought his car to a halt at the side of the road, and watched, fascinated and enthralled, as the glowing ball began to almost rhythmically sway, as if prodded or pushed by a gentle gust of wind. Fascination and enthrallment soon gave way to overpowering fear, however, when the ball quickly moved in his direction, possibly because, the man admitted to both an FBI special-agent from Phoenix and a representative of the Air Force, he had left his car's headlights on and its engine running to ensure no one slammed into the vehicle on the dark and lonely road. "Mr. [Deleted] believes the lights of his vehicle attracted the 'Flying Disc' to his whereabouts," recorded the FBI, in its three-page report on the affair.

Within seconds, the strange object was 50 feet above the car. It was at this point that the engine suddenly died, the headlights were extinguished—both by forces unknown—and the man found himself bathed in a light blue glow that, the FBI noted, "caused [the witness] to develop tingling in his fingers and lips."

Likening the craft to a large "spinning-top," the man told the authorities that as he gazed upward, utterly awestruck, he suddenly developed the distinct thought that the craft was "flown by men from space who are watching us know there is an atom bomb," and added to the interviewing agents that he believed "the space men are here to halt all future wars." Then, in an instant, the UFO was gone: it shot vertically in the sky to a height that the man—as an experienced pilot in the war and as a crop-duster—estimated to be around 600 or 700 feet, at which point "Mr. [Deleted] believes the light was turned off and [the] disk traveled in darkness in an unknown direction" (Federal Bureau of Investigation).

This particular report is highly illuminating as countless people, all across the world since the late 1940s, have claimed face-to-face contact with eerily human-like aliens from far off planets who have expressed concerns about our growing atomic arsenals—just as the witness in this Sedona-based case of 1947 had suggested. These aliens, which have become known as the Space Brothers, are usually seen dressed in tight-fitting, one-piece outfits, and sporting heads of lush, long, and flowing blond hair. Not only that, our cosmic visitors assure those of us who they deem worthy of contact that they are deeply concerned by our violent, warlike ways. They wish us to disarm our nuclear arsenals, live in peace and harmony with one another, and elevate ourselves to whole new spiritual levels. Those whose lives have been touched and forever changed by their encounters with such alleged extraterrestrial entities are an elite group of people known as the Contactees.

If the testimony of the witnesses can be considered valid, then in the early years of contact, the aliens took a decidedly alternative approach to their liaisons with the people of Earth; something which may explain why the military had such a hard time proving the reality of the UFO phenomenon. Allegedly preferring face-to-face encounters with every-day members of society, the Space Brothers arranged their clandes-tine meetings at such out-of-the-way locations as isolated hills, lonely mountains, and…desert canyons. Perhaps, a desert canyon like the very one over which the UFO at Sedona in August 1947 was seen hovering.

Not everyone is quite so sure that all of the perceived UFO encoun-ters in Sedona are the work of aliens from far away worlds that have concerns about our nuclear capabilities. There are those who conclude that they actually have nothing to do with the activities of *real* aliens but are solely the result of clandestine work undertaken by the U.S. military. According to this scenario, the military uses the UFO motif as a care-fully camouflaged cover to allow for the testing of new technologies and classified aircraft, as well as the utilization of mind-controlling drugs, and sophisticated hypnotic techniques on unwitting citizens.

A perfect example is the case of Alison, who lives on a ranch on the fringes of Sedona. From the age of 27 to 31, Alison says she was subjected to at least five abductions that bore all the hallmarks of alien kidnappings. On each occasion, she was in her living room reading or watching television when her two pet dogs—Lucy and Summer—began pacing around the room and whimpering. At that point, things always became a blur and Alison later found herself several hours later in a different part of the house. Grogginess, a pounding headache, and a dry mouth were staples of the experience.

For days after the weird encounters, she dreamed of the moment when things began to go awry, which always resulted in a complete loss of electricity inside the house, a deep humming noise emanating from outside the large living room window, and powerful and intensely bright lights enveloping the room. In her semiconscious state, Alison saw small shadowy figures scuttling around the room that carried her outside onto a small craft where she was subjected to a gynecological examination and some form of nasal probing. She was then returned to another part of the house and the aliens left. It was only after the aliens had departed that the intense humming noise ceased.

During what Alison believes was the fifth abduction, however, something even weirder took place. The mysterious humming sound abruptly came to a halt only a few seconds after her allegedly cosmic visitors entered the room. At that point, Alison recalled—not in a later dream, on this occasion, but in real time—she began to slowly regain her senses and the feeling of disorientation eased and then completely vanished. *And so did the aliens.* In their place was not a group of frail-looking, black-eyed extraterrestrials, but a number of rather large men in what looked like black combat fatigues.

The men, clearly aware that Alison was regaining her senses, backed away slowly and one of them held his hand up as if motioning her not to move as they quickly exited her home. Alison, however, made her way to the window in plenty of time to see the men jump into an un-marked black helicopter and take to the skies. At a height of several hundred feet, a powerful lamp was turned on that that lit up the night-sky around her secluded property for a few moments. So much for a genuine spaceship.

Today, Alison firmly believes that a combination of subliminal hyp-nosis, mind-altering technologies, and perhaps even non-lethal weap-onry designed to temporarily disable her nervous system and bodily movement, made her *think* she was an alien abductee. In reality, how-ever, Alison concludes, she was merely a guinea pig for the testing of sophisticated weaponry designed to affect and manipulate both mind and body to an incredible degree. Sedona, then, may very well be home to mysteries of several varieties: alien, paranormal, supernatural, and military.

From a place of enchantment and vortexes, what could be next? How about a land—and a whole bunch of mysteries—down under?

24

Sydney, Australia

Beyond any shadow of doubt, Sydney can claim fame to having played host to one of the most mystifying and bizarre of all creatures ever encountered. And I do not use those two words—*mystifying* and *bizarre*—lightly. After all, how else would you describe a diminutive beast that looks like an elephant, but walks on its hind legs, and surfaces from the depths of a dark lagoon? That was exactly what a woman named Mabel Walsh encountered in Narrabeen—a beachside suburb of Sydney—back in the late 1960s.

While driving home late one April 1968 evening with her nephew, John, Walsh was shocked to see the approximately 4-foot-tall animal emerge from the watery depths and shuffle its way into the heart of nearby scrubland. It was a creature that Walsh would never forget, even though it was in view for only mere seconds. Gray in color, with what looked like a tough, leathery skin, it had a snout resembling that of an anteater, a slim trunk, long back legs, and a pair of short forelimbs that dangled as it waddled along sideways by the edge of the road before vanishing into the scrub.

The local newspaper, the *Daily Telegraph*, recognizing the publicity the story would surely create, splashed the details across its pages. In an article titled "And Now It's the Monster of Narrabeen! Loch Ness Was Never Like This" the details of Mabel Walsh's story tumbled out, which provoked yet more reports of the fantastic creature. Some of them sounded decidedly sensationalized because they suggested the monster of the deep had taken to dragging sheep, cows, and horses to their hor- rific deaths in the heart of the lagoon; a most unlikely action for a crea- ture barely 4 feet tall! Others spoke in near-hysterical tones of seeing a bright red, clawed hand come out of a hole in the ground at the lake and try to grab a terrified youngster.

The (almost) final word on the matter went to Mabel Walsh, who started the controversy and told newspaper staff that people might call her crazy, but she was absolutely sure there was a bizarre creature in Narrabeen Lake. As it transpired, not many did call her crazy. The *Daily Telegraph's* audience excitedly lapped it all up, and, sales-wise, its staff was very happy indeed. But that wasn't quite the end of the matter. Bill Chalker is a noted Australian UFO researcher and writer who investi- gated a wave of UFO activity that occurred not only at the same time that Sydney's very own Elephant Man appeared, but in the very same place, too. Chalker, who traveled to the area in the late-1970s came up blank, and admitted that there was nothing concrete to directly link the strange creature to the UFOs and mysterious lights that were being seen over and around Sydney. But he did learn that there were other witnesses to the unearthly beast, including a pair of fishermen, who, on an unspecified date late at night, saw a near-identical animal to that encountered by Mabel Walsh, swimming in the water, rather than wad- dling alongside it.

Moving on, but still on the matter of Sydney's resident monsters, we have to now take a trip to the vast and picturesque Blue Mountains. Chiefly composed of a huge plateau that borders Sydney's bustling met- ropolitan area, the mountains sit in the central region of what is known as the Sydney Basin, and are home to one of the area's most famous attractions: a trio of tall peaks known as the Three Sisters. Many, however, claim that the Blue Mountains are home to something even more spectacular than those three rocky women: the Australian equivalent of Sasquatch. Or, as it's known in the land down under: the Yowie. Although skeptics very often suggest that sightings of hairy, man-like entities are primarily, and predominantly, from recent years, this is very far from the case. Within aboriginal lore and mythology, the existence of the hairy man of the Blue Mountains, and of elsewhere in Australia, has been known for centuries.

A report from 1842 provides a good and graphic image of what was widely believed about the creature in earlier years by native aborigines, when it was known as the Yahoo rather than the more popular Yowie of today:

> This being they describe as resembling a man of nearly the same height, with long white hair hanging down from the head over the features, the arms as extraordinarily long, furnished at the extremities with great talons, and the feet turned backwards, so that, on flying from man, the imprint of the foot appears as if the being had travelled in the opposite direction. Altogether, they describe it as a hideous monster of an unearthly character and ape-like appearance. (Anonymous)

Then, 40 years later, came this account from one H.J. McCooey:

> A few days ago I saw one of these strange creatures. I should think that if it were standing perfectly upright it would be nearly five feet high. It was tailless and covered with very long black hair, which was of a dirty red or snuff-color about the throat and breast. Its eyes, which were small and restless, were partly hidden by matted hair that covered its head. I threw a stone at the animal, whereupon it immediately rushed off. ("Australian Apes")

And, today, not much has changed.

Schoolteacher, and Blue Mountains resident, Neil Frost had his very own close encounter of the Yowie sort in February 1993. It was a creature that, perhaps most justifiably, Frost described as looking like an elephant on two legs and wearing size 20 boots. How very apt for a monster whose transatlantic cousin goes by the name of Bigfoot! It was around midnight when Frost woke from his slumber. But, rather than take a trip to the bathroom and risk waking his young son to the sound of flushing water, Frost crept outside and relieved himself in the bushes of the backyard. Out of the shadows and the trees loomed an immense, hair-covered, bipedal creature—one that Frost estimated easily weighed in at 285 pounds—which took off at high speed into the surrounding woods.

Demonstrating a keen flair for adventure, Frost raced around to the home of his neighbor, Ian "Lizard" Price, and breathlessly told him of what had just occurred. The duo was soon off in hot pursuit of the man-thing amongst them. But despite the very best efforts of the pair, and several nights of getting extremely close to finding the beast, during which the pair even found its immense footprints, the blazing-eyed monstrosity always eluded them. Then, as mysteriously as it first appeared, it was forever gone. But, it was certainly never forgotten by Frost and his buddy, Lizard.

Adding even more to the mystery of the Blue Mountains and the westernmost fringes of Sydney—and just as is the case with England's Cannock Chase woods and Rendlesham Forest—they are the reported home to a population of mysterious, large black cats that, quite simply, should not exist anywhere in Australia. In September 2008, Nathan Rees—the Premier of New South Wales, Australia—admitted that he did not believe the big cats of Sydney could be written off as modern-day folklore. This was a far cry indeed from a statement Rees made only one month earlier to the effect that reports of big cats on the loose were merely the stuff of urban legend. Rees's rapid turnaround was hardly surprising, however: He confirmed 600-plus reports collected and collated at a local level had just been brought to his personal attention.

Just such a creature was seen in May 2010 by Paul Cauchi and his girlfriend, Naomi, as they were driving through Yarrawonga. Cauchi said that although the black-colored beast was only in view for a handful of seconds, both he and Naomi were absolutely certain that what they saw was not merely a large feral cat. They were sure it was a panther. Such was the publicity given to the report, even New South

Wales' Minister for Primary Industries, Steve Whan, admitted that other reports of the creature had reached Sydney-based officialdom, and added that the government took all such reports very seriously. As for the question of where the cats may have originated, with down to earth and regular explanations sorely and mysteriously lacking, it has been suggested that perhaps they represent the descendents of melanistic cougars brought to Australia as mascots by U.S. military forces during World War II, and then secretly released into the wild when the Americans headed off to do battle with the Japanese. Certainly, this is a nice theory, but one that falls flat for one specific reason: No solid proof of such a scenario having occurred has ever surfaced.

Sydney, Australia's haunted St. Andrew's Cathedral (copyright unknown, 1900)

When it comes to ghosts and tales of a life after death variety, Sydney—just like Halifax, Nova Scotia—is certainly near the top of the list in terms of quantity. And there is another Halifax parallel, too: In a situation that very closely mirrors the story attached to Halifax's St. Paul's Anglican Church of a haunted pane of glass, a similar tale surfaces from Sydney's St. Andrew's Cathedral, which opened for business in 1868, and just happens to be the oldest cathedral in all of Australia.

The identity of Sydney's glassy specter is unknown, but, for three days in 1932, visitors to the cathedral claimed that one of the windows on the huge east window showed the radiant, side-profile image of what appeared to be a long-haired woman staring upward. And although many—particularly those who worked at the cathedral—were content to dismiss the manifestations as merely the result of shadows distorted by the sun, this was a theory that others found highly dubious because the eerie image was not a permanent fixture, but one that only appeared across a tantalizing period of 72 hours, or thereabouts. The mystery, therefore, lives on.

Far more regularly seen spirits can be found in a series of old buildings collectively called Quarantine Station—where, beginning in 1832, nearly 600 people infected with bubonic plague, smallpox, cholera, Spanish influenza, and numerous other killer diseases, were left to die agonizing and terrifying deaths, after the Australian Government passed the so-called Quarantine Act, in a panicky attempt to halt the racing, disastrous spread of deadly infection across the entire nation. Today, Quarantine Station is a pleasant hotel and restaurant, and, upon visiting it, scarcely anyone would even suspect it had a dark past and an even darker, supernatural present.

One of the more famous ghosts of Quarantine Station, and who flatly refuses to leave—or who, perhaps, is unable to leave—is that of a young, blond-haired girl who, when the National Parks and Wildlife Service holds its regular ghost tours for would-be spook-seekers, enjoys playfully tugging on the sleeves of the curious and captivated throng. Most take no notice of her actions, because they assume she is merely the daughter of one of the other tourists. That is, until they are told no-one under the age of 18 is allowed on the terrifying tour.

Terrible, disembodied screams and shouts have been heard coming from what used to be the hospital ward. Strange balls of floating light—eerily similar to the Nayaga light of the Han River, Vietnam—have been seen wandering the old corridors. Might they, too, just like the Han River light, be the disembodied souls of the restless, tragic dead? Perhaps we should not discard such a controversial theory, given that the ghost light of both locales is intimately, and inextricably, linked to the domain of the afterlife.

Finally on the matter of Quarantine Station: Rather intriguingly, just like Sydney's St. Andrew's Cathedral and Nova Scotia's St. Paul's Anglican Church, it also has a reputedly haunted window. It can be found in the old mortuary and is said to be paranormally etched with the face of an aboriginal man who died in that very room many years ago. Though apparently, not everyone who takes a careful look at the glass is guaranteed to see the man's visage. He is quite picky and choosy when it comes to who he appears for. After all, it must be rather tiring, if not tiresome, to have to perform on cue like a trained dolphin at the zoo every time someone comes along demanding a bit of action. Even the many ghosts of Sydney, it seems, need a bit of down time.

Now it's time for the final stop on our worldwide, weird tour. Are you ready for some monster mayhem?

25

Taushida, Guyana

Guyana is a sovereign state on the northern coast of South America and borders a large percentage of the Caribbean Sea. And for adventurers and thrill-seekers in search of a solid amount of undeniable mystery and mayhem, look no further than this captivating and enigma-filled land. The mountainous areas that surround the little village of Taushida are defined by their beauty, dense jungles, waterfalls, deep caves, luscious foliage, and widely varied wildlife. But, they are also defined by their profound strangeness and menace, too. And for such a small place, the sheer level of downright bizarreness attached to Taushida is extraordinary.

An ancient tiger-like animal that is said to have the uncanny ability to live in, and even *under*, the water of the many rivers of the area is spoken of in whispered, worried tones. The locals claim that their very own equivalent of Bigfoot—the Didi—inhabits the nearby hills. And giant snakes—anacondas, many say—of an incredible 40 to 50 feet in length, and with bodies the widths of oil-drums, coil and slither their

189

terrible way around the land in search of a tasty human or several to satisfy their voracious appetites.

We will begin with that creature of the deep: the Water Tiger, as its name translates to in English. Although very well known to, and deeply feared by, the people of Taushida, the apparent existence of the beast remained largely unknown to outsiders until 2007. In November of that year, a five-person team from Britain's Center for Fortean Zoology (CFZ)—which had heard rumors of the predations of this particularly weird monster of Guyana—embarked upon an ambitious expedition to Taushida, in an effort to finally uncover the truth about the terrors that lurk in and around the small, secluded hamlet. It was during the course of this expedition that one of the team members, Richard Freeman, uncovered a wealth of fascinating information on the Water Tiger. Freeman, formerly a head zookeeper at England's prestigious Twycross Zoo, initially wondered if the legends of the creature were based upon people actually having seen a real animal, but one of a far more down to earth nature: a large type of giant South American otter, *Pteronura brasiliensis*. Having had the opportunity to spend time amongst the people of Taushida and carefully nurture and gain their trust and confidence, however, Freeman's views on the matter changed both quickly and drastically.

Thanks to one of the CFZ's guides on the monster hunt—Kenard Davis—Freeman was introduced to an elderly villager named Elmo who was a wealth of data on this unique creature of the deep. It was data that provided very good reason as to why the Water Tiger was, and to this day still is, so feared at a local level. The mysterious animal, said Elmo, was undeniably a member of the big cat family—it had a spotted coat not unlike that of a Jaguar—but spent most of its time in the river waters of the area, which just happened to be its preferred hunting grounds. The picture painted for Freeman was one of terrifying proportions. The Water Tiger, Elmo explained, was an incredibly vicious killing machine that hunted in packs, and whose overall length was more than 10 feet. Crossing paths with the creature was most definitely not recommended, Freeman was told, in knowing and cautious words.

We have already seen that wild and hairy man-beasts populate several of the places upon which this book focuses, such as the Caucasus Mountains, Eurasia; Rendlesham Forest, England; the Solomon Islands; and Mount Shasta, California. Taushida is no different. For the people of the village, their equivalent of Bigfoot is known as the Didi. The Guyana version is a very curious one indeed, however: its hair is said to be red, rather than the generally reported brown and its fingers are topped off with vicious-looking claws. Apes, however, do not possess claws, which has given rise to the theory that perhaps the Didi is a surviving relic of a giant sloth, *Megatherium* that lived in certain parts of South America up until around 10,500 years ago.

Wild men of the woods abound in Taushida, Guyana (copyright Hans Burgkmair, 500)

Whatever the true nature and origin of the creature, the Center for Fortean Zoology's team uncovered some extraordinary information on this wild thing of the woods. They were told of how, only two or three years earlier, two young children—a girl and a boy, both around 11 or 12—were taking a pleasant stroll across the savannah after school, when suddenly they were plunged into a terrible nightmare from which one never recovered. Out of a large group of nearby trees, a giant, hairy, man-like animal raced across the grassland in the direction of the petri-fied pair. It grabbed the terrified girl and charged away with her at high speed. The girl, tragically, was never seen again.

Possibly of some relevance to the reported existence of the Didi, the CFZ personnel learned—from one Damon Corrie, a chief of the Eagle Clan Arawak Amerindians—of the discovery of what appeared to be huge stone clubs and shields in the mountains. It was a discovery that led Corrie to speculate that perhaps they were fashioned by the Didi, in which case the creature might very possibly be considered something more akin to a primitive man than an unknown type of ape. And then there is the story uncovered by the CFZ that suggests somewhat of a paranormal angle to the mysterious existence and presence of the Didi.

On one particular day back in the 1950s, Richard Freeman was told, Kenard Davis' father was out hunting in the mountains and had been fortunate enough to snare two wild fowl that would surely make a hearty meal for his family that night. While negotiating the treacherous terrain back home, Davis' father was shocked to see a huge, hair-covered man seemingly asleep in what looked like a hammock constructed out of carefully intertwined vines in a large tree. The terrified and awestruck hunter fled for his life, but still kept a tight grip on the evening's din-ner. On returning to the village, however, something most disturbing happened: Quite out of the blue, the man suddenly fell seriously ill. Fearing that the Didi had placed a deadly curse upon him, the acutely scared man quickly consulted the local shaman. After entering a trance state and allegedly having made direct psychic contact with the crea-ture itself, the shaman assured Davis' father this was fortunately not the case. The Didi, said the shaman, had told him that it was merely shock and fear—and not a curse—that had provoked the sudden bout of illness and that, in reality, the Didi were quiet creatures that preferred to live in peace and tranquility in the mountains, far away from the day to day stresses of the human race. And they are not, apparently, the only mysterious hominids that inhabit Taushida.

From Kenard Davis, Richard Freeman learned that, until the 1970s, a population of very curious little fellows lived in the area. They were pigmy-like humans of a primitive, animalistic nature and appearance, only about 3 feet in height, hairless, lacked any form of clothing, and wore red paint on their faces. Possibly of relevance to this story, is the account provided to Freeman of a tribal chief who encountered what sounds just like one of these strange beasts back in the latter years of the 1960s. Although the description of the little man-thing was broadly the same as that of Kenard Davis, the chief told Freeman that, having seen the entity up close and personal, he was sure that what Davis believed was paint on its face was actually a natural pigment of its skin. The Bush People, as the chief referred to them, were not dangerous, kept to themselves deep in the forests, and lived in primitive dwellings built below large trees. Rather notably, just like the hair-covered Kapre of Laguna, in the Philippines, the Bush People of Guyana were said to have a particular liking for tobacco, and would, late at night and in the early hours of the morning, raid nearby homes to steal and partake of their favorite drug.

With tigers of the waters and man-beasts large and small now dissected, whatever next? Well, how about those giant, marauding snakes? The Center for Fortean Zoology's team discovered, sightings had been made of an absolutely vast anaconda inhabiting a large pool adjacent to the Corona Falls only one year prior to their November 2007 expedition. This was a true monster, one with a thick, wide body, possibly in excess of 40 feet in length, and it was seen coiling itself around a large tree by horrified hunters. Rather than ending up as dinner themselves, they took the wise choice of fleeing the area, fortunately unseen and unscathed by the slithering monstrosity.

Nearby Crane Pond, potentially the lair of such an immense anaconda, has a notable legend attached to it: *Don't sleep too deeply at Crane Pond or the dragon will take you.* And there is a very good reason for that warning, too. One night back in the 1950s, and at a time when cattle-ranching was still very big business in the area, a group of cowboys chose to camp on the edge of the pond after a hard day's work in the field. They probably wished, with hindsight, that they headed straight for home. In the middle of the night, they were all suddenly woken by the loud splashing, and even louder breathing, of something huge and foul slowly surfacing from the depths of the pond. Unbridled fear and calamity broke out. Guns were fired wildly in the darkness, horses were hastily rounded up, and each and every one of the hunters fled before the tables were turned and they became hunted by the nightmare of Crane Pond.

Richard Freeman wondered if the monster could have been a huge anaconda. Very possibly, for the following reason that Freeman, an expert on reptiles, astutely notes: "Anacondas do make a strange sound when breathing, which has been likened to snoring." Although Freeman and the team did not see evidence of an anaconda 40 feet in length, they did stumble upon several anaconda trails during their time in the area—deep furrows filled with water—that were suggestive of creatures close to 20 feet long. And with snakes of that size slithering among the savannah, falls, and ponds, one might be very wise to take careful steps when negotiating the land. The team also came across a story with somewhat of a conspiratorial aspect attached to it. In Taushida in the late 1990s, an English hunter supposedly shot and killed a vast anaconda, at least 30 feet long. The man, locals said, in quiet and careful tones, was a powerful figure with a lot of influential connections at an official level who secretly and illegally shipped the skin of the snake to Britain and to the hunter's very own private collection of prized animal hides (Freeman).

And, finally—to demonstrate that, just like so many other areas of the world that have been addressed so far, Taushida is steeped in strangeness of more than just one nature—Richard Freeman collected several stories during his trip of people seeing strange lights and UFOs hovering over the Taushida Mountains; in some cases, only weeks before the Center for Fortean Zoology embarked upon its expedition. One such report, from early 2007, involved four hunters who, late one night while tracking animals for food, saw a large, black, triangular-shaped

UFO hanging briefly in the air, and in complete silence, near the base of the mountains, but which shot away in equal silence and at a fantastic speed into the star-filled heavens. And a second told of a small, white-colored, egg-shaped UFO seen briefly flying at low level over the savannah in July 2007.

Truly, Taushida and its surroundings amount to a collective prehistoric world of the type made famous in Michael Crichton's *Jurassic Park* and Sir Arthur Conan Doyle's *The Lost World*. Hollywood fiction, it might justifiably be said, isn't always fiction, after all.

Conclusion

Our journey into the depths of the world's weirdest places is at its end. None can deny that our trek has been long, winding, and decidedly strange. It's not enough, however, to simply record the fact that our planet seems to have far more than its fair share of specific areas that act as veritable magnets for mysterious events; strange creatures; UFOs and aliens; enigmatic entities, such as fairies and goblins; and an absolute multiplicity of spectral figures of a wide and dizzying nature. The bigger question that requires a solid answer is surely this: Why, exactly, do these magnet-like beacons for all things supernatural even exist in the first place? We start with what have become known, in paranormal circles, as window areas.

Loren Coleman, one of the world's leading experts on strange creatures and unidentified animals, says of this very issue:

> Certain areas appear to be routinely visited by Fortean
> events. Depending upon your interests, these locales

may be called "haunted places," "monster countries," "spook light sites," "triangles," or "windows." John Keel [the author of *The Mothman Prophecies*, among many acclaimed titles] created the concept and indeed coined the word, as well as certainly popularizing the notion of "windows…"

Jerome Clark, an authority on all-things-weird, notes of Keel and window areas that:

> The phenomena [Keel] records, exemplify the window at its bizarre best: Over a period of many months UFO activity is frequent, sometimes so frequent that people go UFO-hunting on a nightly basis with reasonable expectations of sighting something. The sightings include events ranging from distant observations to close encounters. Paranormal activity of other sorts often amplifies as well; the Point Pleasant area was also a hotbed for encounters with men in black and a monstrous creature known as Mothman. This full panoply of phenomena accompanies some long-term, narrow-distribution waves; in others the window opens wide enough to admit only UFOs.

But are window areas forever destined to remain unexplained and languish in the domain of what is vaguely defined as the supernatural and the paranormal? Perhaps not: It's now that we turn our attention to what are known in particle physics-based research as wormholes. Imagine a kind of cosmic version of New York's subway system, or London's sprawling underground railway. Just like its terrestrial equivalents, the cosmic variety allows you to jump on at one point and get off at another of your personal choosing. But, this one also allows you to do something else, too; something unique and astonishing. Namely, it provides you with the ability to completely bypass the cumbersome and time-consuming major problem of having to travel from Point A to Point B in linear, minute-by-minute fashion.

In essence, a wormhole is a theoretical shortcut that has the ability to cut a definitive swathe through the very fabric of both space and time, not unlike the scenario famously portrayed in the 1994 movie *Stargate*, starring Kurt Russell and James Spader. In the movie, the U.S. military secretly deciphers a series of codes and hieroglyphics adorned on a huge, ancient, stone ring found at Giza, Egypt, back in 1928—codes and hieroglyphics that turn out to be coordinates for faraway stars and galaxies. And, by entering those same coordinates into the Stargate, the universe is, quite literally opened up to Uncle Sam.

This is an issue elaborated upon and echoed by Marie D. Jones, whose book *PSIence*, extensively researches the issue of wormholes:

> Traveling through a wormhole would not, as many people might think, mean going faster than the speed of light. In fact, wormholes don't require light speed at all. It is the time that it takes to travel through the hole that gives the impression of faster-than-light travel. All you really need is a black hole and a white hole and you have your own personal Stargate. The black hole serves as the entry point, and the white hole, the exit. (Jones)

There's one particular type of wormhole called the Lorentzian Traversable Wormhole that may play a role in all this. Physicists speculate Lorentzian Traversable Wormholes might not only permit travel from one part of the universe to another, but also at an incredibly fast rate of speed, and possibly even instantaneously, too—thus supporting the conclusions of Marie Jones. Moreover, the two points of connection may very possibly be static, stable, and unchanging. In other words, we would have a situation where strange entities from strange worlds, realms, and dimensions—entities possibly deeply adept and skilled at negotiating our very plane of existence via the advanced science of wormholes—might pop up time and time again at certain, specific locales on our planet. Those same locales could allow for potential permanent connection with the domains of the mysterious others that have for so long been staple parts of our culture, history, mythologies, folklore, religions, and belief-systems, and perceived variously as aliens, demons, monsters, gods, or as countless other paranormal conundrums.

And as Marie D. Jones suggests, the phenomenon of wormholes may also help to solve one of the mysteries that consistently turn up in the pages of *The World's Weirdest Places*: ghosts. Jones says of such ethereal entities: "Ghosts that seemingly have the ability to interact with their witnesses might be actual entities coming through from other dimensions and universes, via wormholes of some sort, or portals that allow for the synching up of their world and ours" (Machado).

Supernatural portals, galactic gateways, windows to other worlds, stepping-off points for unearthly entities, or wormholes: Call them what you will, but it's hard to deny they offer a viable and logical solution for the existence of what are, undeniably, the world's weirdest places and the enigmatic, eerie, amazing, fantastic, and always elusive things—whether alien-like, monstrous, or spectral—that dwell within their mysterious hearts.

Bibliography

"About Mount Shasta." *www.siskiyous.edu/shasta/fol/lem/index.htm*, 2003–2009.

"Aleister Crowley's Birthday." *www.visitlochness.com/events/Aleister-Crowley-Birthday.php*, 2012.

Anderson-Forbes, Rob. "British Military Fishing Expedition Spots Sea Serpent Off Nova Scotia Coast." *www.mystrangeblog.com/2010/08/british-military-fishing-expedition.html*, August 16, 2010.

Andrew. "Carew Cheriton Control Tower: World War 2." *www.carewcheritoncontroltower.co.uk/history*, December 16, 2010.

Anon. Letter to *Australian and New Zealand Monthly Magazine*, Vol. 1, No 2, February 1842.

"Are There a Tribe of Cavemen Living Under Cannock Chase?" *www.sundaymercury.net/news/midlands-news/2008/08/14/are-there-a-tribe-of-cavemen-living-underneath-cannock-chase-66331-21537130/*, August 14, 2008.

Aspinall, Adam. "Cannock Chase Murderer Raymond Leslie Morris breaks 42 year silence." *www.sundaymercury.net/news/ midlands-news/2011/04/17/cannock-chase-murderer-raymond-leslie-morris-breaks-42-year-silence-66331-28532942/*, April 17, 2011.

"Australian Apes." *Australian Town and Country Journal*, December 9, 1882.

"Background Note: Philippines." *www.state.gov/r/pa/ei/bgn/2794. htm#history*, January 17, 2012.

Bagge, Sverre. *Society and Politics in Snorri Sturloson's Heimskringla*. Berkeley, Calif.: University of California Press, 1991.

"Bala Lake." *www.snowdoniaguide.com/lake_bala.html*, 2005–2006.

Bateman, Wes. *Knowledge from the Stars*. Flagstaff, Ariz.: Light Technology Publications, 1993.

Bennett, Colin. "John Whiteside Parsons." *Fortean Times*, March 2000.

Berg, Daniel. *Bermuda Shipwrecks*. East Rockaway, New York: Aqua Explorers, 2000.

Berlitz, Charles. *The Bermuda Triangle*. New York: Doubleday, 1974.

———. *The Dragon's Triangle*. New York: Fawcett, 1991.

"Bhangarh." *www.thedimensionzone.com/paranormal/most_haunted_ bhangarh.htm*, 2008–2011.

"Bhangarh, India." *www.dorsetghostinvestigators.com/#/bhangarh-india/4556062001*, 2012.

"Big Cats Seen In Eyke in 2003?" *Ipswich Evening Star*, October 16, 2003.

Bjornsson, Sveinn Birkir. "Chasing Monsters in East-Iceland." *www. grapevine.is/Travel/ReadArticle/Chasing-Monsters-in-East-Iceland*, September 5, 2008.

Blanco, Juan Ignacio. "Mack Ray Edwards." *www.murderpedia.org/ male.E/e/edwards-mack-ray.htm*, 2012.

Boirayon, Marius. "The Giants of the Solomon Islands and Their Hidden UFO Bases." *www.thewatcherfiles.com/giants/ solomon-giants.htm*, 2012.

———. *Solomon Islands Mysteries*. Kempton, Ill.: Adventures Unlimited Press, 2010.

"Brown Mountain Lights." *www.brownmountainlights.com/*, 2000–2011.

Butler, Brenda, Dot Street, and Jenny Randles. *Sky Crash: A Cosmic Conspiracy.* London: Grafton, 1986.

"Caddo Lake State Park." *www.tpwd.state.tx.us/spdest/findadest/parks/caddo_lake/*, 2012.

Cahill, Tim. "Death Valley." *http://ngm.nationalgeographic.com/2007/11/death-valley/cahill- text/1*, November 2007.

"Cannock Chase German War Cemetery, Staffordshire, England." *www.ww1cemeteries.com/british_cemeteries_memorials_ext/cannock_german_cem.htm*, 2012.

"Cannock Chase—Werewolves." *www.ghost-story.co.uk/stories/annockchase.html.* May 15, 2010.

"Cannock Forest." *www.forestry.gov.uk/cannockforest*, 2012.

Capps, Chris. "Ghosts of the Soviet Union Still Haunt Kremlin." *www.unexplainable.net/ghost-paranormal/the-ghosts-of-the-soviet-union.php*, January 17, 2012.

Carey, Thomas J. and Donald R. Schmitt. *Witness to Roswell.* Pompton Plains, N.J.: New Page Books, 2009.

Carter, John. *Sex and Rockets: The Occult World of Jack Parsons.* Port Townsend, Wash.: Feral House, 1999.

Casscass. "The Quarantine Station Tour." *www.yourghoststories.com/real-ghost-story.php?story=1518*, July 16, 2007.

"Caucasus Mountains." *www.peakbagger.com/range.aspx?rid=38*, 2012.

Cerny, Paul C., and Robert Neville. "U.S. Navy 1942 Sighting." *www.waterufo.net/item.php?id=1113*, 2012.

"CFZ Guyana Expedition, 2007." *http://cfzguyana.blogspot.com/*, 2012.

"Charles Webster Leadbeater, His Life, Writings and Theosophical Teachings." *http://blavatskyarchives.com/leadbeaterbib.htm*, 2008.

Chase Reporter. "Chase Beast's Getting Bolder." *Chase Post*, March 2, 2000.

Chester, Keith. *Strange Company: Military Encounters with UFOs in WWII.* Charlottesville, Va.: Anomalist Books, 2007.

Childress, David Hatcher. *Lost Cities of North and Central America*, Kempton, Ill.: Adventures Unlimited Press, 1992.

"City of Jefferson." *www.visitjeffersontexas.com/*, 2009.

Clark, Jerome. *High Strangeness*. Detroit, Mich.: Omnigraphics, 1996.

Clarke, Dr. David. "Spook Lights." *http://drdavidclarke.co.uk/spooklights/*, 2012.

Coleman, Loren. "Alligators in the Sewers are Real." *www.cryptomundo.com/cryptozoo-news/sewers-gators-real/*, November 26, 2006.

———. *Mothman and Other Curious Encounters*. New York: Paraview Press, 2002.

———. "Nessie Footage Questions Focus on Filmmaker." *www.cryptomundo.com/cryptozoo-news/holmes-concern/*, June 4, 2007.

———. "Solomon Islands' Giants." *www.cryptomundo.com/cryptozoo-news/solomons-giants/*, October 28, 2010.

Counter-Intelligence Corps, U.S. Air Force Office of Special Investigations. *Unidentified Flying Object: Lagarfljot River, Northeastern Iceland*. October 11, 1954.

Courtney, Margaret Ann. *Cornish Feasts and Folk-Lore*. Lanham, Md.: Rowman & Littlefield, 1973.

Crawford, Lois, J. "Our Beloved Messenger: Guy W. Ballard." *www.lcrawfords-manymansions.com/Ascended%20Master%20Instruction/Guy%20Ballard/Guy%20Ballard%202.htm*, 2012.

"Creature spotted on Mt. Shasta." *Mount Shasta Herald*, September 9, 1976.

"Death Valley National Park." *www.desertusa.com/dv/du_dvpmain.html*, 2012.

"Death Valley National Park." *www.nps.gov/deva/index.htm*, 2012.

Dickinson, Peter. *The Flight of Dragons*. New York: HarperCollins, 1981.

Diimaan. "Haunted Bhangarh Fort: The Ghost Town of Rajasthan." *http://thinkingparticle.com/articles/haunted-bhangarh-fort-ghost-town-rajasthan*, January 6, 2011.

"Dining with Ghosts from the Titanic." *www.tastefortravel.com.au/blog/4833/dining-with-ghosts-from-the-titanic/*, April 11, 2012.

"Discovering the Kremlin." *http://archive.kremlin.ru/eng/articles/history_00.shtml*, 2012.

Dodd, Tony. *Alien Investigator*. London, England: Headline, 1999.

Dongo, Tom. *Everything You Wanted to Know About Sedona in a Nutshell.* Flagstaff, Ariz.: Light Technology Publications, 1998.

———. *Mysterious Sedona.* Flagstaff, Ariz.: Light Technology Publications, 2000.

———. *The Mysteries of Sedona.* Flagstaff, Ariz.: Light Technology Publications, 1998.

Downes, Jonathan. "Richard Freeman: More About the Red Faced Dwarfs..." *http://cfzguyana.blogspot.com/2007/11/richard-freeman-more-about-red-faced.html,* November 26, 2007.

Doyle, Arthur Conan. *The Hound of the Baskervilles.* London, England: George Newnes, 1902.

"Dragon River Bridge, Da Nang, Vietnam." *www.roadtraffic-technology.com/projects/dragonriverbridge/,* 2011.

"Dragon's Triangle (Devil's Sea)." *www.paranormal-encyclopedia.com/d/dragons-triangle/,* 2012.

Drummond, Allan. *The Wild Man of Orford.* Wivenhoe, England: Jardine Press Ltd., 1995.

Eberhart, George M. *Mysterious Creatures: A Guide to Cryptozoology.* Santa Barbara, Calif.: ABC-CLIO, 2002.

Emery, David. "Alligators in the Sewers." *http://urbanlegends.about.com/od/alligators/a/sewer_gators.htm,* 2012.

Farwell, Lisa. *Haunted Texas Vacations.* Englewood, Colo.: Westcliffe Publishers, 2000.

Faulk, Odie B. *The U.S. Camel Corps: An Army Experiment.* New York: Oxford University Press, 1976.

Federal Bureau of Investigation. *Flying Disk, Sedona, Arizona,* August 17, 1947. Declassified under the terms of the U.S. Freedom of Information Act.

Feindt, Carl W. *UFOs and Water.* Bloomington, Ind.: Xlibris, 2010.

Ferguson, Wes. "Bigfoot hunter trusts his nose to find creature." *Longview News Journal,* October 17, 2004.

"Five Fishermen Restaurant and Grill." *www.fivefishermen.com,* 2012.

Freeman, Richard. "The Bogey Men of the Philippines." *The Center for Fortean Zoology 2011 Yearbook* (edited by Jonathan and Corinna Downes). Woolsery, England: CFZ Press, 2011.

———. *CFZ Expedition Report: Guyana 2007.* Woolsery, England: CFZ Press, 2008.

———. *CFZ Expedition Report: Russia 2008*. Woolsery, England: CFZ Press, 2008.

———. "In the Coils of the Naga." *www.cfz.org.uk/ expeditions/00naga/naga1.htm*, 2012.

"Ghost Cases." *www.redstarfilmtv.com/ghostcases.php*, 2012.

"'Ghost Cases.' The Five Fishermen." *www.imdb.com/title/tt1749789/ combined*, 2012.

"Ghosts of Roswell, The." *www.coasttocoastam.com/show/2004/02/26*, February 26, 2004.

"Ghosts of the Kremlin." *http://hauntedearthghostvideos.blogspot. com/2012/04/ghosts-of-kremlin.html*, April 12, 2012.

Gibbons, Gavin. *By Spaceship to the Moon*. Oxford, England: Blackwell Publishers, 1958.

Glasgow Boy. "The First Book on Nessie." *http://lochnessmystery. blogspot.com/2011/01/first-book-on-nessie.html*, January 9, 2011.

Gracia, Anton, D. "Aswang—Pinoy Supernatural Creatures." *www. thepinoywarrior.com/2011/10/aswang-pinoy-supernatural-creatures.html*, October 21, 2011.

Gray, Jonathan. "Does a Giant Race Still Exist in the Solomon Islands?" *www.beforeus.com/giant_solomons.html*, 2012.

Group, David. *The Evidence for the Bermuda Triangle*. Wellingborough, England: Aquarian Press, 1984.

Gruber, Barbara. "Iceland: Searching for Elves and Hidden People." *www.dw.de/dw/article/0,,2786922,00.html*, June 2007.

Gunnell, Terry. "Gryla, Grylur, Groleks and Skelkers." *http://jol. ismennt.is/english/gryla-terry-gunnell.htm*, 2012.

Hacker, Simon. "Days Out: The shy monster of Bala lake." *www. independent.co.uk/travel/news-and-advice/days-out-the-shy-monster-of-bala-lake-662073.html*, February 24, 2002.

"Halifax." *www.halifaxinfo.com/*, 2005.

"Halifax Connection." *http://titanic.gov.ns.ca/connection.asp*, 2012.

"Halifax Explosion, The." *www.cbc.ca/halifaxexplosion/*, 2012.

"Halifax Sea Serpent." *http://unmyst3.blogspot.com/2010/10/halifax-sea-serpent.html*, October 15, 2010.

"Halifax to Remember the Titanic With Night of Bells Ceremony." *www.cbc.ca/news/canada/nova-scotia/story/2012/04/14/ns-halifax-titanic-night-of-bells.html*, April 14, 2012.

Halpenny, Bruce Barrymore. *Ghost Stations IV: True Ghost Stories.* Chester-le-Street, England: Casdec, 1991.

Halt, Lieutenant Colonel Charles E. *Unexplained Lights.* United States Air Force, January 13, 1981.

"Han River Bridge in DaNang—Vietnam." *http://vietnamtravelfaq. com/2009/03/10/han-river-bridge-in-danang-vietnam/,* March 10, 2009.

"Haunted Places in Roswell, New Mexico." *http://hauntin.gs/New%20 Mexico/Roswell/,* 2012.

Healy, Tony & Cropper, Paul. *The Yowie: The Search for Australia's Bigfoot.* Charlottesville, VA: Anomalist Books, 2006.

Henry, Lori. "Haunted Places: The Five Fishermen in Halifax, Nova Scotia." *http://lorihenry.ca/10/haunted-places-the-five-fishermen-in-halifax-nova-scotia/,* October 15, 2010.

"Historic Jefferson TX Ghost Walk." *www.jeffersonghostwalk.com/,* 2009–2012.

"History of Halifax." *www.halifaxkiosk.com/history.php,* 2012.

Holiday, F.W. *The Dragon and the Disc.* London, England: Sidgwick & Jackson, 1973.

———. *The Great Orm of Loch Ness.* London, England: Faber, 1968.

"Humanoid Elephants: (Australia)." *www.americanmonsters.com/ site/2011/06/humanoid-elephants-australia/,* June 7, 2011.

"Iceland Mythology: Elves, Trolls and the Hidden People." *www. icelandinsider.com/mythology.html,* 2012.

"Icelandic Town Hopes Angry Elves Have Been Soothed by Songs." *www.icenews.is/index.php/2011/07/02/icelandic-town-hopes-angry-elves-have-been-soothed-by-songs/,* July 2, 2011.

"Icelandic Trolls." *www.icelandtoday.is/DiscoverIceland/Superstition/ IcelandicTrolls/,* 2012.

"Icelandic Wonders: Elves, Trolls and Northern Lights!" *www. icelandicwonders.com/Default.asp?Page=240,* 2012.

"Inverness Man Reports Puma-Like Sighting." *www.thefrasers.com/ nessie/news/nesspapr090801.html,* September 8, 2001.

Ishabtr. "Ruins of Bhangarh—The Haunted Village of Rajasthan, India." *www.traveldudes.org/travel-tips/ruins-bhangarh-haunted-village-rajasthan-india/14777,* November 28, 2011.

Jacobsen, Annie. *Area 51: An Uncensored History of America's Top Secret Military Base.* New York: Little, Brown & Company, 2011.

"Japan's Dragon's Triangle." *www.unexplainedstuff.com/Places-of-Mystery-and-Power/Japan-s-Dragon-s-Triangle.html,* 2012.

"Jefferson Hotel, The." *www.ghostinmysuitcase.com/places/jeffhotel/index.htm,* 2001-2006.

"Jefferson, Texas." *www.jefferson-texas.com/,* 2000–2007.

Jeffrey, Adi-Kent Thomas. *The Bermuda Triangle.* New York: Warner, 1975.

"Jet Propulsion Laboratory: Early History." *www.jpl.nasa.gov/jplhistory/early/index.php,* 2012.

Jim H. "The Sailing Stones of Death Valley." *http://historicmysteries. com/sailing-stones,* April 25, 2010.

Johanek, David. "Death Valley's Lost City." *http://home.rconnect. com/~arcanaresearch/id6.html,* 2005.

Jones, Marie D. *PSIence: How New Discoveries in Quantum Physics and New Science May Explain the Existence of Paranormal Phenomena.* Pompton Plains, N.J.: New Page Books, 2006.

Jones, Richard. *Haunted Castles of Britain and Ireland.* New York: Barnes & Noble Books, 2003.

Jones, T. Gwynn. *Welsh Folklore and Folk-Custom.* London, England: Methuen & Co., 1930.

Keel, John A. *The Mothman Prophecies.* New York: Tor, 1991.

Kelbie, Paul. "For sale on Loch Ness: Aleister Crowley's Center of Dark Sorcery." *www.guardian.co.uk/uk/2009/apr/19/boleskin-bay-sale-satanism,* April 18, 2009.

Kimball, Paul. "High Strangeness in Halifax." *http://redstarfilms. blogspot.com/2005/10/high-strangeness-in-halifax.html,* October 19, 2005.

Kitz, Janet F. "The Halifax Explosion." *http://museum.gov.ns.ca/mma/atoz/HalExpl.html,* December 6, 2008.

"Klamath Indian Legends." *http://oe.oregonexplorer.info/craterlake/history.html,* 2012.

"Kremlin Ghosts Are Alive and Kicking." *http://rt.com/art-and-culture/news/kremlin-ghosts-are-alive-and-kicking/,* December 27, 2008.

Kusche, Lawrence David. *The Bermuda Triangle Mystery Solved.* Amherst, NY: Prometheus Books, 1975.

"Laguna Islands, Philippines. 'Resort Province of the Philippines.'" *http://laguna.islandsphilippines.com/*, 2012.

Lang, Ruby, and Michael Williams. "Yowieland—A Window Into Australia's Bigfoot Enigma." *http://web.mac.com/rebeccalang/ Strange_Nation/Yowieland.html*, 2012.

Lansdale, Edward Geary. *In the Midst of Wars*. New York: Fordham University Press, 1991.

Lee, Bourke. *Death Valley*, New York: Macmillan Co., 1930.

———. *Death Valley Men*, New York: Macmillan Co., 1932.

LeMay, John. *Images of America: Roswell*. Mount Pleasant, S.C.: Arcadia Publishing, 2008.

Lesley, Lewis Burt (Ed.). *Uncle Sam's Camels: the Journal of May Humphreys Stacey, Supplemented by the Report of Edward Fitzgerald Beale*. San Marino, Calif.: Huntington Library Press, 2006.

Machado, Karina. "Q and A with Marie D. Jones." *http:// karinamachado.com/guest-interviews/q-a-with-marie-d-jones/*, 2012.

Macleod, Calum. "Big Cat Sightings Spark Lambing Time Farm Alert." *Inverness Courier*, May 2, 2000.

Mahoney, Mack. Letter to Frank Edwards, February 3, 1962.

Man, John. *Kublai Khan: The Mongol King who Remade China*. New York: Bantam Press, 2007.

"Marfa Lights Research." *www.nightorbs.net/*, March 22, 2012.

Marrs, Jim. "Alien Ghosts at Roswell?" *http://aliencats.multiply.com/ journal/item/1115/Aliens_And_Ghost_At_Roswell?&show_inte rstitial=1&u=%2Fjournal%2Fitem*, October 17, 2009.

Marrs, Jim. *PSI Spies*. Pompton Plains, N.J.: New Page Books, 2007.

Marshall, Tom. "The Belen Cemetery: A Riveting Combination of History & Legend." *http://marshalltom.wordpress. com/2010/07/23/the-belen-cemetery-a-riveting-combination-of- history-legend/*, July 23, 2010.

McCormick, Kylie. "Dragons of Fame: Agunua / Hatuibwari." *www.blackdrago.com/fame/agunua.htm*, November 9, 2010.

Messina, Paula. "The Sliding Rocks of Racetrack Playa." *http://geosun.sjsu.edu/paula/rtp/intro.html*, 2012.

Miller, Andrei. "Magical Creatures and Non-Human Beings of the Philippines." *www.mysiquijor.com/MagicCreatures.html*, 2002–2007.

Miller, John Maurice. *Philippine Folklore Stories*. Whitefish, Mont.: Kessinger Publishing, 2004.

Morgan, Tom. "The German Cemetery at Cannock Chase, Staffordshire." *www.fylde.demon.co.uk/cannock.htm*, 1997.

Mt. Shasta, Peter. "Mount Shasta and the New Shambala." *www.mountshastamagazine.com/mystique/*, 2000–2011.

"Mount Shasta Sighting, The." *www.thecryptocrew.com/2012/01/mount-shasta-sighting.html*, January 28, 2012.

"Narrabeen's mysterious elephant man." *www.cfzaustralia.com/2011/10/narrabeens-mysterious-elephant-man.html*, October 21, 2011.

"New York City Subway System." *www.nycsubway.org/*, 2012.

Nicolson, E. "Ghosts of the 1917 Halifax Explosion." *http://enicolson.hubpages.com/hub/Ghosts-of-the-Halifax-Explosion-1917*, 2012.

O'Neal, Leo H. "The Legend of the Death Valley Mummies." *Far Out*, Vol.1, No.2, Winter 1992.

"On the hunt for the big cat that refuses to die." *www.cfzaustralia.com/2010/06/on-hunt-for-big-cat-that-refuses-to-die.html*, June 20, 2010.

"Origin of the Lemurian Legend, The." *www.siskiyous.edu/shasta/fol/lem/index.htm*, 2012.

"Original 'I AM' Instruction: How it all Began." *www.saintgermainfoundation.org/*, 2012.

"Panteon de Belen Haunted Cemetery Legends." *www.explore-guadalajara.com/hauntedcemetery.html*, 2012.

Parsons, Chris. "Russian Protesters Distracted During Moscow Demo Against Putin...by 'UFO' fFlying Over Kremlin." *www.dailymail.co.uk/news/article-2073132/Russian-protesters-distracted-UFO-Moscow-demo-Vladimir-Putin.html*, December 13, 2011.

"Pasadena's Suicide Bridge." *www.weirdca.com/location.php?location=57*, April 8, 2009.

Pavils, Gatis. "Naga Fireballs of Mekong." *www.wondermondo.com/Countries/As/Thailand/NongKhai/NagaFireballs.htm*, September 23, 2010.

Pendle, George. "Jack Parsons and the Curious Tale of Rocketry in the 1930s." *www.thenakedscientists.com/HTML/articles/article/Georgependlecolumn1.htm*, March 2006.

Pendle, George. *Strange Angel: The Otherworldly Life of Rocket Scientist John Whiteside Parsons.* San Diego, Calif.: Harcourt, 2005.

Pharand, P., *Unidentified Flying Objects.* Bedford Highway Patrol, Royal Canadian Mounted Police, October 27, 1976.

Phoenix, Silver. "Legend of the Yule Cat." *www.angelfire.com/moon/phoenixhearth/ponderings/yulecat.html*, 2012.

Picknett, Lynn. *The Loch Ness Monster.* Stroud, England: Pitkin Guides, 1998.

Pippin, Jerry. "City of Spirits: The Hauntings of Jefferson, Texas." *www.jerrypippin.com/Paranormal_Jefferson_Ghosts.htm*, 2012.

"Premier Sinks Claws Into Big Cat Mystery." *www.cfzaustralia.com/2008/09/premier-sinks-claws-into-big-cat.html*, September 20, 2008.

PSICAN Group. "Halifax Sea Serpent." *http://psican.org/alpha/index.php?/Nova-Scotia-Cryptozoology/Halifax-Sea-Serpent.html*, 2012.

"Q Station: Adult Ghost Tour." *www.qstation.com.au/experience/tours.php*, 2012.

"Quarantine Station, North Head, Manly." *www.castleofspirits.com/quarantine.html*, 2012.

"Rajasthan's 'Ghost' Town Bhangarh Now a Popular Tourist Spot." *http://articles.timesofindia.indiatimes.com/2010-08-21/india/28318033_1_ghost-town-ghost-story-tantrik*, August 21, 2010.

Randolph, Octavia. "Huldufolk—the Hidden Folk, and Trolls." *www.octavia.net/vikings/huldufolk.htm*, 2012.

Raynor, Dick. "Loch Ness Video by Gordon Holmes May 2007." *www.lochnessinvestigation.com/gordonholmes2007video.htm*, March 31, 2010.

Redfern, Nick. *Body Snatchers in the Desert.* New York: Simon & Schuster, 2005.

———. "CFZ: The Russian Wildman." *http://monsterusa.blogspot.com/2008/12/cfz-russian-wildman.html*, December 10, 2008.

————. "CFZ Zoologist Richard Freeman on the Search for Monsters in Guyana." *http://monsterusa.blogspot.com/2007/10/cfz-zoologist-richard-freeman-on-search.html*, October 25, 2007.

————. *Cosmic Crashes.* London, England: Simon & Schuster, 1999.

————. "Do Werewolves Roam the Woods of England?" *http://monsterusa.blogspot.com/2007/05/do-werewolves-roam-woods-of-england.html*, May 17, 2007.

————. "Enter the Dragon Hunter." *Space Girl Dead on Spaghetti Junction.* Woolsery, England: CFZ Press, 2011.

————. "Freeman and Russian Man-Beasts." *http://monsterusa.blogspot.com/2011/04/freeman-russian-man-beasts.html*, April 13, 2011.

————. "In Search of the Last Mammoth." *Darklore*, Volume 5. Brisbane, Australia: Daily Grail Publishing, 2010.

————. "Monsters of the Mountains: Hunting the Russian Bigfoot." *www.mania.com/lair-beasts-monster-mountains_article_111257.html*, November 22, 2008.

————. "More on Area 51, Roswell, Jacobsen, Etc." *http://desertdarkness.blogspot.com/2011/05/more-on-area-51-roswell-jacobsen-etc.html*, May 31, 2011

————. "Richard Freeman: An Exclusive Interview on the Beasts of Guyana." *http://monsterusa.blogspot.com/2007/12/richard-freeman-exclusive-interview-on.html*, December 13, 2007.

————. "The CFZ, the Almasty, and the Russian Expedition: The Press Release." *http://monsterusa.blogspot.com/2008/06/cfz-almasty-and-russian-expedition.html*, June 9, 2008.

————. "A New York Monster: The Creature of the Park." *www.mania.com/lair-beasts-new-york-monster_article_118724.html*, November 7, 2009.

————. "The Monster of the Pool." *http://nickspicoftheday.blogspot.com/2011/11/monster-of-pool.html*, November 4, 2011.

————. *Wild Man!* Woolsery, England: CFZ Press, 2012.

"Rendlesham Forest Centre." *www.forestry.gov.uk/rendlesham*, 2012.

Rhys, John. *Celtic Folklore.* Charleston, S.C.: Forgotten Books, 2007.

Roberts, Andy. *UFO Down!* Woolsery, England: CFZ Press, 2010.

Rochak. "Bhangarh: The most haunted place in India." *http://mystic-places.blogspot.com/2007/07/bhangarh-most-haunted-place-in-india.html*, July 24, 2007.

Ronquillo, Ulysses. "Aleister Crowley at Boleskine House." *http://weird-people.com/aleister-crowley/*, 2012.

"Sailing Stones of Death Valley." *www.psiro.com/index.php/articles/paranormal-news-a-stories/86-sailing-stones-of-death-valley.html*, 2012.

"Roswell, New Mexico." *www.seeroswell.com/*, 2012.

"Roswell, New Mexico Ghost Sightings." *www.ghostsofamerica.com/8/New_Mexico_Roswell_ghost_sightings.html*, 2012.

"Saint Andrew's Cathedral, Sydney, Australia." *www.sydneycathedral.com/*, 2010.

Saint Germain Foundation. *The History of the "I AM" Activity and Saint Germain Foundation.* Schaumburg, Ill.: Saint Germain Press, 2003.

Salla, Michael. "Pravda hides link between Kremlin UFO pyramid and Norway light spiral." *www.examiner.com/article/pravda-hides-link-between-kremlin-ufo-pyramid-norway-light-spiral*, December 19, 2009.

"Scary Ghost Stories and Spooky Tales from the Panteon de Belen." *www.explore-guadalajara.com/scaryghoststories.html*, 2012.

Scott-Elliot, W. *Lost Lemuria, The.* Charleston, S.C.: Forgotten Books, 2007.

"Sea Serpent" Sighting. 315th Air Command Group, September 19, 1965.

Soderlind, Rolf. "Elves in Modern Iceland." *www.ismennt.is/vefir/ari/alfar/alandslag/aelvesmod.htm*, 2012.

"Solomon Giants UFO Update." *http://solomongiants.wordpress.com/2011/02/05/si-government-seriously-considers-ufos/*, February 5, 2011.

Spencer, John Wallace. *Limbo of the Lost.* New York: Bantam, 1969.

"Stanzas of Dzyan, The." *http://blavatskyarchives.com/dzyan.htm*, 2012.

"Strange and Unexplained—Hollow Earth." *www.skygaze.com/content/strange/HollowEarth.shtml*, 2012.

Stringfield, Leonard. *UFO Crash/Retrievals: The Inner Sanctum.* Cincinnati, Ohio: Published privately, July 1991.

"Suffolk Beast Spotted Again." *www.edp24.co.uk/news/suffolk_beast_spotted_again_1_115540?ot=archant.PrintFriendlyPageLayout.ot*, August 10, 2007.

Sulzberger, A.G. "The Book Behind the Sewer-Alligator Legend." *http://cityroom.blogs.nytimes.com/2009/11/23/the-book-behind-the-sewer-alligator-legend/*, November 23, 2009.

Sutphen, Dick. *Sedona: Psychic Energy Vortexes.* Scottsdale, Ariz.: Valley of the Sun Publishing Company, 1994.

Tabitca. "Teggie the Welsh Lake Monster and a Crocodile." *http://cryptozoo-oscity.blogspot.com/2009/04/teggie-welsh-lake-monster-and-crocodile.html*, April 21, 2009.

Tanner, Mabel. Letter to Raymond A. Palmer, August 30, 1949.

"Teddy May Page, The." *www.sewergator.com/people/teddy_may.htm*, 2012.

Thomas, Jeffrey, L. "Carew Castle." *www.castlewales.com/carew.html*, 2009.

Thomas, Lars. *Weird Waters: The Lake and Sea Monsters of Scandinavia and the Baltic States.* Woolsery, England: CFZ Press, 2011.

"Titanic's Connection to Nova Scotia." *www.novascotia.com/en/home/discovernovascotia/history/titanic/default.aspx*, 2012.

Towrie, Sigurd. "The Wild Hunt." *www.orkneyjar.com/tradition/hunt.htm*, 1996-2012.

"Trace of Giants Found in Desert." *Associated Press*, August 4, 1947.

Trubshaw, Bob. *Explore Phantom Black Dogs.* Avebury, England: Heart of Albion Press, 2007.

Tucker, Duncan. "Mozart, Vampires and Graveyards at Night." *http://guadalajarareporter.com/features-mainmenu-95/908-features/29925-mozart-vampires-and-graveyards-at-night.html*, November 4, 2011.

"UFO Pyramid Reported Over Kremlin." *www.telegraph.co.uk/news/newstopics/howaboutthat/ufo/6837200/UFO-pyramid-reported-over-Kremlin.html*, December 18, 2009.

Unidentified Flying Objects, Project "Grudge" Technical Report. Air Materiel Command, U.S. Air Force, 1949.

"Vampire Ghost in Guadalajara." *http://vampiremoviefan.com/81/vampire-ghost-in-guadalajara/*, July 27, 2011.

Vernon, Steve. *Halifax Haunts: Exploring the City's Spookiest Places.* Halifax, Nova Scotia: Nimbus Publishing Ltd., 2009.

"Visit Cannock Chase." *www.visitcannockchase.co.uk/*, 2012.

"Visit Iceland." *www.icelandtouristboard.com/index.php?page=About-Iceland*, 2009.

"Wales Lake Bala Monster Teggie." *http://cryptoreports.com/wales-lake-bala-monster-teggie*, April 3, 2012.

Warren, Larry, and Peter Robbins. *Left at East Gate*. New York: Marlowe & Company, 1997.

Weiser, Kathy. "California Legends: Suicide Bridge on Route 66." *www.legendsofamerica.com/ca-suicidebridge.html*, February 2010.

Weiss, Janna. "The Most Haunted Hotel in Texas." *http://voices.yahoo.com/the-most-haunted-hotel-texas-572315.html*, October 3, 2007.

"When Did Maximilian von Herff Die?" *www.trueknowledge.com/q/when_did_maximilian_von_herff_die*, 2012.

"Wild Man of Orford, The." *http://myths.e2bn.org/mythsandlegends/origins63-the-wild-man-of-orford.html*, 2006.

"Wild Man of Orford, The." *www.orfordmuseum.org.uk/panel4.html*, 2012.

Winton, Ellis P. "Lemurian Encounter on Mount Shasta." *http://onelight.com/telos/wintonellis.htm*, 2012.

Witchell, Nicholas. *The Loch Ness Story*. London, England: Corgi Books, 1982.

Wood, Ryan S. *Majic Eyes Only*. Broomfield, Colo.: Wood Enterprises, 2005.

Woolheater, Craig. "Bigfoot in Texas?" *http://forteanswest.com/lowfiguesteditorial-CraigWoolheater0909.html*, 2009–2010.

Worley, Don. "The Winged Lady in Black." *Flying Saucer Review, Case Histories*, No. 10, June 1972.

Yancey, Diane. *Camels for Uncle Sam*. Dallas, Tex.: Hendrick-Long Publishing Co., 1995.

"Yule Lads, The." *www.simnet.is/gullis/jo/yule_lads.htm*, 2012.

"Yule Lads, The." *www.thjodminjasafn.is/english/for-visitors/christmas/the-yule-lads/*, 2012.

Zanger, Michael. *Mt. Shasta: History, Legend, Lore*. Berkeley, Calif.: Celestial Arts, 1992.

Index

About the Author

Nick Redfern works full-time as an author, lecturer, and journalist. He writes about a wide range of unsolved mysteries, including Bigfoot, the Loch Ness Monster, alien encounters, UFOs, and government conspiracies. His previous books include *The Pyramids and the Pentagon*; *Keep Out!*; *The Real Men in Black*; *The NASA Conspiracies*; *Contactees*; and *Memoirs of a Monster Hunter*. He writes for many publications, including *UFO Magazine*; *Fate*; and *Fortean Times*.

Nick has appeared on numerous television shows, including Fox News; History Channel's *Ancient Aliens*, *Monster Quest*, and *UFO Hunters*; VH1's *Legend Hunters*; National Geographic Channel's *The Truth about UFOs* and *Paranatural*; BBC's *Out of this World*; MSNBC's *Countdown*; and SyFy Channel's *Proof Positive*. He can be contacted at *http://nickredfernfortean.blogspot.com*.

Other Titles From
NEW PAGE BOOKS